My Grandmother's Diary

Fiorella Palomino Andrade

My grandmother's diary

First edition: 2024

To my mother, the Bella of my life.

Contents

Prologue

It has taken me almost three years to decide to write this book; I cannot deny that I felt like I was baring my thoughts in doing so, but my love for writing has triumphed in this battle, in which boldness dethroned decorum, allowing me to express myself freely.

Next, dear reader, you will delve into the world of Perla, who will take you on a journey to discover some secrets of the Martini family, written during the pandemic. Along this path, she will fill the pages of this book with her personal concerns, typical of the moment in her life when the story takes place. Moreover, you will travel through different settings, as this work is set in various parts of the world. You will move through time with Perla to uncover different episodes in the life of this family, primarily focusing on the family's anchor: Grandmother Isabella Martini.

You will also learn about the values that shaped this family, as well as the imprints they left on each of its members—values that would later become the fuel for the engine of their lives. I try to capture in these lines the respect and admiration I feel for many people around me; the story of each of them has been my motivation to write. I also attempt to express my enthusiasm for life, and I hope to share with my readers at least a little bit of my love for what has been, my fascination with the present, and my desire for all of us to find a way to leave our mark on this world. I hope you can sense some of my sensitivity in each chapter, as I have put a little piece of my heart into them.

This is my first book; I present it so you can learn about the story of this woman who, without realizing it, finds her own path by delving into her grandmother's past.

Finally, I want to encourage you to master your fears. I am somewhat pusillanimous, I always say; however, this has never hindered me. On the contrary, I have taken my fears by the hand everywhere, and they were the ones that encouraged me the most when I needed it.

The Author

I. The Illness

March 3, 2020

"BESAME MUCHO" I was greeted at Miami airport by a sort of sign made of what looked like a bouquet of colorful flowers in shades of pink, with that phrase written on it. I spent just over five hours on the plane that brought me directly to Florida, a tiring and tedious flight from Denver, Colorado, to spend a few days with my grandmother Isabella before her operation. Isabella is my paternal grandmother, whom I have not seen in about two years, but we talk on the phone quite often.

She has been living alone for many years in a small yet cozy apartment; from the terrace, overlooking a lake, you can see beautiful sunsets. It is located in Broward County, in the city of Weston, about forty minutes by car from Miami airport.

Isabella's operation, as she told me, is scheduled for March 14. Since my return to Colorado is planned for the 12th of the same month, I will not be able to stay with her for the operation. However, we have arranged for a nurse to accompany her during the first month after the surgery to assist in her recovery. After that,

Gabo, my father, will come to spend some time with her, followed by my aunts Alba, Alondra, and Paloma taking turns. I will try to return during that time, but I am not entirely sure if the dates will work out as I hope.

Lately, I have been extremely busy at the clinic with the children I attend to. They are more open than ever to sharing their thoughts, fears, and experiences; they express themselves more easily. I am not sure if it is the time we spend together that makes them feel more confident with me or if it is me being more persistent in applying the techniques I have been studying. In any case, I feel like we are making substantial progress with most of the kids.

All of this keeps me quite occupied, although I think a lot about Charlie, my dog, who passed away a few weeks ago. My dear Charlie was with me for sixteen years. He was small, with round eyes, white, with long fur, very handsome, and of no particular breed. I adopted him on a trip my dad and I took to Cancun when I was thirteen to celebrate his birthday. We found him alone on the street, young (he must have been about two months old), hungry, and thirsty. I did not plan to take him with me, but days later, we had him in a special basket we bought for him, flying back home with us. I adored Charlie from the moment I saw him. It is definitely true what they say about dogs: we do not save them; they save us. Charlie saved me so many times that my heart aches every time I think he is no longer with me; I feel a little piece of me die remembering his eyes when we said goodbye. I could not say goodbye because I did not want him to go, but he, with his gaze, told me we would meet again.

It is because of him that I started writing this kind of diary to help me channel these confusing feelings between sadness and remorse because I feel like Charlie dedicated almost his entire life to me, while I, on the other hand, owed him the last few months. I focused only on work and Javier, my boyfriend. I neglected Charlie's care even though I knew he was sick and these might be his last months with me.

And so it happened. One night at home, while I was sitting at the computer working on some reports, Charlie became ill. Suddenly, I had to check on him in his bed, and when I approached, I saw he was struggling to breathe and whimpering softly. I immediately took him to the clinic, but his last moments were upon us. The vet advised me to say goodbye, that it was better to let him go, but that it was important for him that I be by his side at that moment. I cannot understand why I hesitated; sometimes, I wonder how I could have considered not going in to hold his paw. I guess it was my way of trying to avoid that pain, but in the end, I went in. I stayed with him in his last moments without speaking, unable to utter a single word, just holding his gaze throughout. I was not ready, definitely. His passing hurts me deeply.

I have so much to tell... I also want to write about Javier and the relationship we are currently in. I am not sure how it started, but what is worse, I am not sure if it will end well because his way of thinking and acting is so different from mine. I understand we do not have to be the same, but I confess I wish we had at least some things in common. His reaction, for instance, to Charlie's passing has been so cold. At times, it seemed like it was something he had been expecting so that he would not have to share my time with anyone else. I am incredibly surprised to see such a strange and evident calmness in him, although he knows how hard all of this has been for me. However, I love him, and I know he loves me too; he shows it in his own way, maybe not the way I would like, but I understand everyone has a unique way of loving.

The day has been quite long. I hope to get to Bella's house quickly because I am quite tired. Jane, my secretary, confirmed she arranged for a taxi to pick me up at the airport exit. I will call her to find out what is happening, as the taxi has not arrived yet, and I want to get to Bella's before she goes to bed; I would not want her to worry or be inconvenienced by having to wake up for me. Besides, I am on a tight schedule to prepare my presentation for the event on March 13. This annual activity is of utmost importance, as I invite psychologists from various parts of the world to donate hours of work as volunteers at the clinic for children, where I am a founding partner and practice as a psychologist. I emphasize my responsibility for this event, as the success of this conference affects the recovery of young patients who cannot afford treatment at the clinic. I need to draft my speech in a way that convinces these professionals to donate some hours of their busy days to the proposed cause. Essentially, it is about giving their time to people who can only repay their work with gratitude, gaining the satisfaction of having helped a family overcome a crisis.

Although this sounds beautiful in theory and should be very motivating for our profession, in practice, it is not, and the duty to achieve this falls on me.

This year, we have an ambitious target to meet, and I am confident we will reach it. I am going for it!

March 10, 2020

My grandmother's apartment is just as I remembered it. As you open the main door, you enter the living room, which is perfect for my taste; the most beautiful picture is painted on the way to the terrace, overlooking the lake. With such a spectacle, no additional decoration is needed in this part of the house, and it seems Bella agrees, as the décor in this space is understated. My grandmother has always loved plants, which is evident in every corner of her home.

There are two bedrooms, each with its own bathroom. The master bedroom is where my grandmother sleeps, and the other room is for family and friends who come to Florida to enjoy the warmth and visit Bella. The dining room is where action happens in my grandmother's house: simple, white, clean, and orderly. It's where we always gather all those who visit her home. Family meals have always been especially important, during which we come closer to each other and show affection.

That is how Bella was raised in her home since she was young, and that's how Bella raised her children, so that today, after four generations, we continue the Martini family tradition. At the dining table, the most important decisions are made, the best moments are celebrated, and the deepest sorrows are cried out—there, in that room of the house.

I have spent many hours with my grandmother these days. We have talked about everything, even about my good Charlie, about how much I miss him, about how much I loved him.

Bella showed me beautiful photos of the entire family that I had forgotten. I even found some pictures of me with Charlie when he was a baby. I cried; she comforted me. With that comfort, I remembered how wonderful it feels to be listened to and to receive a sincere hug. It is strange; it seems to me that I have not felt like this in several months, or even years, despite living with my boyfriend.

I will take one of the baby pictures of Charlie with me to Colorado; I want to put it in a beautiful frame that I bought on a trip to Europe last year. I have been keeping it without really knowing why, although Javier wanted to print a photo of us to put there, claiming it was a beautiful memory. I am sure he will understand that I want to use it for my photo with Charlie and will not oppose that; at least, that is what I hope.

Today, I helped Bella organize her kitchen, as there were places she, due to her age, could not reach, and they were slightly disordered. We ate delicious food, and she also gave me a family recipe book. I am eager to get home and start preparing dishes from that book; I am sure Javier, whose family is Spanish, will be happy to know that I have these Italian recipes and will feel at least somewhat closer to his European roots.

At times, I feel like I already want to be back home, even though I have some things there to sort out that I left lying around, especially Charlie's things that I could not bring myself to take. I am not sure if I am ready to part with them, but at least I know I am ready to pack them away; I have even thought about giving them away. I'll take my time and look for a dog shelter to take all his things there; yes, that's what I'll do as soon as I get back home, but first, I have to wait for the conference dates at the clinic to pass so I can start looking for a place to make my donation.

March 11, 2020

I am incredibly anxious; I feel like my heart is about to leap out of my mouth. Today, I do not know how to calm myself down; none of my usual techniques are helping right now. I have been on the phone all day; my flight is tomorrow morning, and we just heard something on the news that I cannot quite comprehend. I had to call Jane, my secretary and friend, my dad, my aunts, and even Javier to discuss the matter. In my mind, everything is clear only up to the moment Bella shouts my name to come to her room; she wants me to watch the television and hear what they are saying.

"Perlaaaa, come quick, listen to this!"

All flights have been canceled until further notice. All public and private recreational places are closed. Hospitals will only handle strictly severe cases and emergencies. Only people with essential jobs, such as those in health care, transportation, and security, among other specified fields, are allowed to leave their homes.

A global pandemic has been declared following the deaths of a considerable number of people worldwide from the coronavirus.

We are unclear about what is happening or how long this situation will last. Everyone has different information about where it started, how the virus spreads, what measures we need to take, what the symptoms are to know if we have the disease and a thousand other questions racing through my mind uncontrollably.

I must call Jane to change my flight; we also need to reschedule the conference, contact everyone who bought tickets, help them cancel their hotel reservations, etc. I am worried everything will fall apart; I am nervous; my fingers will not stop moving, like when I am on the verge of an anxiety attack. I have turned on my computer to start writing these lines just because I need to move my fingers; everything is swirling in my head.

I need to calm down, not just for myself but for Bella. I do not want to make her more nervous than she already is about the upcoming surgery. That reminds me, I need to talk to her doctor and find out what is going to happen with her operation, although I do not really understand what exactly she is being operated for. I never bothered to ask much about this topic or why she needs surgery. Now, I am struck by a new doubt: will her surgery qualify as one of those that can be performed under these circumstances?

I spoke with Aunt Alba, Bella's eldest child. She always has good advice to give; even in the toughest times, she has an answer to every question one might ask. However, this time, I heard from her for the first time:

"I do not know what we will do, dear; we will have to wait a few days to see what happens and how this issue, which is new to everyone, develops."

I then spoke with my dad. He is in Colombia right now; there has not been any lockdown order there yet; at least nothing official has been mentioned, although people are talking on the streets about what is happening here in the United States and other parts of the world.

Naturally, he was overly concerned. He told me to buy him a ticket to fly to Florida as soon as possible; he hopes that being an American citizen will allow him to enter the country and be with Bella and me.

I must sleep; it is almost 1 a.m. here. Bella went to bed over two hours ago; I hope she can sleep peacefully. "There's nothing you or I can do today; just wait. Rest, Perla," were my dad's words.

March 18, 2020

It has been a week since the news came that would change all my plans; I am still in the process of adapting to everything that is happening. I cannot help but feel selfish to think that I am the only one affected by this news in this house. It is my grandmother who encourages me when I am about to overflow with so many unanswered questions; it is astonishing that being eighty-nine years old, she never ceases to amaze me every day.

A few days before this pandemic, I met a Canadian couple, Mr. Thomas and his wife Dorothy, Bella's neighbors. During their extremely cold winters in Canada, they move to Florida in search of eternal summer. They are both in their eighties, but they look great. They invited Bella over for dinner as they usually do, and upon learning I was visiting, they invited me too. I tend to pay attention to how people decorate their homes; it is not to criticize or make comments; it is just my way of trying to get to know them by creating stories about them in my head. Sometimes, my theories about the lives of the owners turn out to be true; other times, they are wrong.

We entered their home, and it wanted to step into the summer patio section of a department store. The entire house was decorated with beach-themed ornaments: seashells on the living room tables, palm trees in the paintings, transparent boxes filled with sand that read phrases like "We love Vero Beach," "I love Florida Beach

Time," and similar things. I felt like I was on a mini-summer vacation.

For dinner, our neighbors ordered pasta from a nearby Italian restaurant that Bella also frequents; they know our family's love for pasta. The food was not bad, but nothing like Bella's pasta recipes. As she always says after finishing her own preparations, *"Boccato di cardinale, figlia mia,"* I suppose they used to say that in her home when she was young, so she nostalgically repeats it after a delicious meal.

I remember something Bella said during that dinner when she saw me looking a bit down. She noticed my mind was wandering at that moment and whispered to me:

"Often, the idea we most try to avoid is the one that pursues us the most."

She said this while holding my hand as we waited for dessert, which had a delightful aroma that spread throughout the dining room, if not the entire apartment. It was a strawberry tart baked by the host, and we devoured it as if it were the last tart of our lives; I left not even a crumb on the plate.

Returning to Bella's phrase that has been haunting me these days, I recalled the paradox of the polar bear phenomenon. This is summed up in what Fyodor Dostoyevsky wrote:

"Try to impose on yourself the task of not thinking about a polar bear, and you will see the damn animal every minute."

That is exactly what is happening to me—an intrusive thought about this disease. The quest for answers is tormenting me; I must find a way to calm my mind.

Before going to bed, I talked with Bella about resuming the meditation that accompanied me for a long time. Unfortunately, I abandoned it when Charlie got sick, replacing it with excessive work because I clearly didn't want to face the idea of staying home to watch the life of my faithful companion of the last sixteen years fade away; I wasn't ready for that moment, and I wanted to avoid it.

Likewise, I told myself I needed to start looking for some physical activity, but only to the extent that home safety is not compromised, as it would be terrible to bring the virus and infect Bella. Today, I'm going to talk to Jane; we'll see what ideas she's found regarding some type of exercise as I asked her to help me find something to do while waiting for the airports to reopen so I can return to my life in Colorado, where I can resume my yoga studio subscription near home that I love so much.

Once in bed, I called Javier; we talked for a while. I think.

I was feeling bad because I had been quite stingy with my feelings towards him. With all this news, I have only been worrying about myself and my plans without considering what he is going through right now.

"Hello, my love, how are you? I am calling not only to greet you but also to say that I am sorry this madness is happening and that we are so far apart. I hope all this gets resolved soon so I can travel back home to be with you."

"Perla, my love, I miss you too, and I want to see you not just on a screen but face-to-face, to be able to touch you and feel you beside me. These days are tough, and without you by my side, they are even tougher. I hope this all passes quickly, too."

"For now, all we can do is wait, but let us not get melancholic. Tell me how everything is at home, how you are planning to continue working in your office, what the plans are..."

March 20, 2020

- Italy, with 3,405 deaths, surpasses China in pandemic fatalities.
- We need help; we are overwhelmed.
- Spain could reach 2.5 million infected in the coming days.
- Confinement is extended for several weeks in distinct parts of the world.
- The healthcare system is on the brink of collapse in China.
- Hospitals are preparing to restrict access to ventilators for the elderly. Priority will be given to young patients with better chances of survival.
- Femicide attacks increase within homes due to the lockdown in Mexico.
- The President of the United States urges people to be responsible and stay home, if possible.

- Argentina orders mandatory quarantine for the entire national territory.

We woke up to these headlines in newspapers around the world; I wanted to write them down so that I will never forget that we are going through this phase in our lives. I am starting to think more clearly now, and little by little, we are getting organized at home with Bella. It is clear that I will not be able to leave here for at least another month, so I have designed a schedule to work on my computer in the room I've shifted, with a small desk and a dining chair. I spoke with Jane, and for now, we have started video calls every morning; it helps us feel a bit like we are in the office. The first ones were very strange; initially, we did them in our pajamas, but now we have decided to dress better, style our hair, and try to make that small morning meeting a bit more formal so we do not lose the habit. We are slowly adjusting to this new routine.

I have enthusiastically resumed meditations. Before starting my workday, I go to the terrace facing the lake and meditate for fifteen or twenty minutes. Sometimes, Bella sits quietly beside me; I sense her presence because she shines even when my eyes are closed. Bella is always a light.

I downloaded a yoga app and started practicing it every night before bed. It helps me a lot; I feel very calm after the class. I have also thought about going for walks some mornings on the golf course next to Bella's building; I noticed there are few people there, which will be good, so I will not come across many others and will not be afraid of getting infected, although we still have to wear masks. Yesterday, our first order arrived by mail. I bought two boxes to ensure we would not run out because they are scarce in local supermarkets now. Sometimes, I find myself wearing a mask inside the house; when I realize it, I quickly take it off and feel the air in my lungs in a unique way. Now, I appreciate so much being able to breathe without something covering half of my face. Bella's phrases and sayings come to mind again; one of them always repeats to me: "One knows what one has; of course, one knows. It's just that we take for granted that it will never be lacking; when we lose it, that's when it hurts, and everything takes on another meaning."

March 21, 2020

What a long day today has been. I finally spoke with Bella's doctor. What a beautiful voice that man has! As we talked, I wondered how old he might be and what his wife would be like if he had children. It was strange. Now that we are locked up and it is difficult to see fresh faces, we question different things.

The doctor explained to me that Bella has a blocked heart vein, needing a minor intervention that is quick and routinely done; this would clean the vein and place a bridge where the blockage is to allow better blood flow. However, due to her advanced age, he did not find it suitable to operate, but Bella insisted, telling him that if she were to die, it would be while eating or swimming in the pool, not from heart pain.

"Your grandmother is a very brave woman, strong and enthusiastic. She manages herself and makes her decisions on her own. She insisted we proceed with the intervention, so we have decided to do it." He said.

We respect my grandmother's decision to undergo the intervention, but as the doctor explained, it is currently not possible due to hospitals and clinics being overwhelmed with pandemic patients, so it is better not to expose ourselves to these places for now. He mentioned he would call Bella in a week to follow up on her case, so I proposed that the communication could be via video call; my suggestion surprised him a bit, but he agreed. I think it would be particularly good for Bella to see the face of the doctor she trusts so much.

In the afternoon, the doorbell rang through the intercom; it was the building security guard asking if we had a dog that was crying. We informed him we did not have dogs, but Bella's neighbors did, although we had not heard anything. So, I offered to go out to see what was happening with the Canadian neighbors' dog. I knocked on their door for thirty minutes. I started gently, but no one answered, so I knocked louder, knowing the neighbors should be home as they were elderly and should not be out on the streets with everything going on. After peering through the window and seeing the dog barking incessantly, I realized something might be wrong. I called 911 to report that my elderly neighbors were not answering the door, and their dog had been alone inside for who knows how long. A few minutes later, firefighters arrived and forced open the door. Ten minutes later, they carried out the two elderly in stretchers; I offered to take care of the dog while they sorted out the neighbors' situation; later, I regretted it, but it was too late: I already had the furry one in my arms.

When I asked what happened, they told me Mr. Thomas had passed away, and Mrs. Dorothy had fainted. Apparently, Mr. Thomas slipped in the shower and fell, and the impact killed him. Upon realizing what had happened, Mrs. Dorothy fainted from shock. That is why the dog would not stop barking and crying to alert the neighbors of what was happening. The firefighters took both elderly people away, though to separate places, but they both left the building together. I stayed with Mr. Marlei, the ten-year-old dachshund, small, with tiny legs and a shy tail. Mr. Marlei is afraid of everything. According to Bella, it might be because Dorothy always overprotects him, not even letting him get off the bed alone for fear of his tiny legs breaking.

As the day ended, I realized I had not written anything about Javier here, although we have been talking regularly. I find it strange, perhaps bored from not being able to go out; he is always highly active and social, and this pandemic must be affecting him a lot; moreover, his work is difficult with these circumstances. Today, talking with Bella, I realized I am not really clear on what Javier does; we have been together for four years, even planning to get married, but I am not sure what his job entails; whenever I ask, it is always complicated to understand. I only know he is a political advisor. He graduated as a lawyer from Duke University in North Carolina, one of the best universities for this career in the United States. Javier is a bit reserved about his cases; in contrast, I love discussing my progress, my patients, and so on. I have thought that when all this madness passes, I will talk more with him about his work; I want to know exactly what he does, who he works for, and what his goals and projects are. Who knows, maybe I can even help him.

Overall, everyone in my boyfriend's family is reserved; I know little about them. For example, I know his father is also a lawyer by profession and came to this country young, at sixteen or seventeen. He studied here and met Javier's mother at university; they married and had two children, one of whom is my boyfriend. Sometimes, I find Javier's father a bit rough, even macho; his mother, on the other hand, looks very calm, quiet, and relatively simple in her dress, unlike Javier's father, who always wears designer suits and smells quite good at any time of day. Javier carries the same name as his father; I do not remember well, but it seems Javier Sr. is about the same age as my Gabo, but they are so different. Gabo is a gentleman through and through, as I always describe him, so polite, sensitive, loving, and sweet as candy; in fact, I think I will not write more for today because if I start writing about my dad, I will spend too much praising him; he deserves it all.

Perla, my dear—Gabo always says to me—you know, there is a phrase that has been etched in my brain since I read C.S. Lewis: 'Education without values, no matter how useful it is, seems rather to make man a cleverer devil.'

As time goes by, this phrase only becomes more accurate, and Gabo becomes dearer to my heart.

Throughout the day, I have been persistently thinking about writing in the upcoming pages about Bella's life. I want to detail what I know about her, as well as ask her some additional questions to confirm the information I already have about her family, our family. Navigating the waters of Martini will be interesting.

March 23, 2020

Approaching her ninetieth birthday next June, from an Italian family that migrated to Peru in 1920 after the end of World War I, Bella, as we affectionately call Isabella Martini in the family, always used to tell us stories about her parents and grandparents in Italy, for whom she would say a prayer every time she mentioned them, showing great respect and deep love.

They were from the coastal city of San Remo, whose shores bathe in the waters of the Mediterranean Sea, northeast of Italy, bordering France. They migrated to Peru by boat in search of better opportunities after the devastating aftermath of the Great War.

Bella's father, Antonio Martini, decided to establish a new life on the other side of the world and brought with him his young wife, Agostina Martini, and Agostina's parents, Mr. Lorenzo and Mrs. Grazia, who lived with the Martini family until their last breaths.

Bella was born in Peru on June 5, 1931, the only daughter of the Martini marriage. It must have been for this reason that both her parents and grandparents raised her like a princess, showering her with love, care, education, and everything else they could provide.

From Bella's lips, I always heard stories of grand feasts at her parents' house, with exquisite homemade pasta whose aroma and flavor still made her eyes and mouth water when recalled. Dishes like *buridda de mariscos*, rabbit stew—when they could get one—and *sardenaira*, which she always repeated, were the mother of what we now know as pizza. All of this was always accompanied by good wine, mostly white, which brightened the long, well-dressed tables for every occasion that Mrs. Grazia took care to arrange for the delight of the whole family. The Martinis, every Saturday during dinner, talked about the adventures of the week, their future plans, family anecdotes, and relatives in San Remo, among other varied topics that emerged as the hours passed and the wine glasses emptied, sometimes well into the night or, on some occasions, into the early hours of Sunday.

They were a closely knit family that treated each other with respect and great manners, always starting each sentence with "please" and ending it with "thank you."

During the carnivals of 1952, celebrated in Lima in February, Bella's grandmother fell ill with what seemed like the simple flu to everyone. Within days, she was bedridden, and the beloved *nonna*, as Isabella called her grandmother, Mrs. Grazia, never recovered.

Nonna passed away on the first day of March from complications of pneumonia, finally diagnosed by the doctor, a disease that attacked her without giving her a chance. That same week, out of pure sorrow, *nonno* also passed away. Mr. Lorenzo could not bear the pain of losing his greatest love, his companion, his friend, and everything, as he always emphasized publicly and privately.

That day, Bella internalized what love would mean to her—the kind that unites and gives life, the kind that stays forever, making it hard to play cards without the missing piece or, in *nonno's* case, no longer yearning for it. Bella then wished to love someday like that, not only to love but also to feel loved in that way. From that day on, love became clearer to her: it is beautiful, it is good, it is honest, and it grows over time.

That same year, at twenty-one, Bella would have met her first husband. She married months after her grandparents' deaths, pregnant with her first daughter. The wedding was simple and intimate, attended only by family and close friends because the loss of her grandparents was still fresh, and Bella's pregnancy made her fragile. These circumstances did not allow for much celebration for the newlyweds.

Five years after her grandparents' deaths, Bella began saying goodbye to her parents: first, her mother, Agostina Martini, her daughter's companion and best friend from the beginning to the end of her days. When Bella talks about death, she always says, "Deaths are always a painful moment, leaving us in a cloud wondering what comes next and why what happened."

Three years after Agostina Martini's death, and already having met two of her granddaughters, Bella's husband, Antonio Martini, passed away in a hospital bed, having lost the battle to prostate cancer that was just beginning to be recognized at that time. He died beside his daughter with the peace of knowing that he left her and his granddaughters financially stable thanks to his efforts in his youth, as well as filled with love and affection.

Antonio would be the most challenging loss in Bella's life. After he departed this world, she felt completely alone. Her life took a turn, but she learned that she could and had an obligation to smile, to keep going even with her heart shattered into a thousand pieces, because time, the best healer there is, would gradually mend it. Time truly heals everything.

After her parents' deaths, Bella was financially stable due to the inheritance left by her parents, which helped her cope with widowhood at a youthful age, a story I will detail later.

In addition to the money her parents left her, they also made sure she received an education. "Education, Bella, will be the lifebuoy we leave you, and someday you'll understand," they would repeat. Therefore, they made sure she attended "girls' schools with a bright future," as they put it, and ahead of their time, they encouraged her to pursue a university degree. Not to mention how emotionally strong and mature Bella always was. Based on my experience as a psychologist, I can say that positive family relationships influenced her, as well as the dedication and love her grandparents and parents had for her. This, undoubtedly, was the foundation that allowed Bella to navigate everything life had in store for her, both the good and the not-so-good.

Isabella, or Bella to us, married three times; from these marriages, she had four children: three daughters and one son, whom she named "Gabriel," as she strongly believes in angels.

My grandmother is a physically beautiful woman; in her young photos, I always see her with long black hair, round, expressive black eyes, a mischievous and captivating gaze, and a big smile, always cheerful.

"Bella" could not have been a better name for her, and you do not just have to look at her to know it, but you also have to know her spirit. After spending some time trying to understand her, any man would have fallen in love with her, unknowingly captivated by her brave soul, boundless heart, sensitivity to listen, and wisdom to speak. I suppose this last virtue is the result of the experiences life gave her and the years she carries with her today, which allow her to be who she is.

My grandmother migrated to the United States at almost forty years old; fifty-four years have passed since the Martini family migrated to the United States in 1966. With a bit more luck than many other migrants of those times who arrived in the country without economic means, education, or knowledge of the language, Bella came to the country with a substantial financial cushion that allowed her to make the down payment for her first house in the state of New Jersey, buy a car, and also pay ahead on some installments of the loan she took out to buy her home.

Later, Bella found a job as a receptionist for a hotel chain, which allowed her to develop a professional career in the tourism and hospitality sector that, over time, would take her to travel to many cities in the United States.

However, although it may not seem like it, Bella was running away from something, from a pain she tried to leave forgotten in the country where she was born, but she would later understand it wasn't about forgetting; on the contrary, she would learn to honor it as one of the most important treasures she would have, to then forge her new path in a different country with a new culture for her, a place she found not difficult to conquer given her always optimistic nature and courage to face life.

In her role as a grandmother, I must be honest that I missed many years with her, as life took me to separate places, partly to know, partly to understand, partly to grow, and partly to experience. It is incredible how true the saying Bella always sings is: "What's meant for you, even if they try to take it away."

I think being here today, accompanying Bella, collecting her memories, and writing this journal had to happen, and I am sure it is the right moment, the perfect circumstance.

This is all I know, in summary, about the life of this woman who still shines wherever she goes, who always leaves me speechless in every detail, from whom I am relearning, and if the word exists and I'm allowed to use it, who is being magic for my days in this pandemic. In the coming days, I will try to ask her details of her life that have escaped my memory or that I perhaps never fully knew, like the story of the early widowhood of my older aunt's father or the love story with my aunt Paloma's father, whom I know passed away a few years ago, or even that of my father's father, whom I never met and know very little about, although I recently heard at a family gathering that he's still alive, but he was never spoken about at home.

March 24, 2020

"Can you see me, Dr. Friedman?" Bella asked.

"Yes, I see both of you." Replied to Dr. Friedman.

"Hello, doctor. It is great to hear you and even greater to see you. It feels like it has been so long. Look, let me introduce you to my granddaughter, Perla. Perla, come closer so the doctor can see you."

"Isabella, do not worry; I can see her. She does not need to come closer to the screen. Nice to meet you, Perla."

"Pleasure is mine, doctor."

"Now, tell me about yourself, Isabella. How have you been feeling these days? How is that brave heart of yours?"

From then on, it was all blah, blah, blah to my ears. My mind drifted again; for some reason, I became distracted by this man's voice. I could only think, "Wow, this doctor could have been a good singer, maybe even an opera singer. Yes, he looks like he would enjoy opera. He would look very dashing in a suit." Then, I started daydreaming about a thousand other things, wondering why he chose the medical profession. I remember when I was little and used to play with Jane, my current secretary, who has been my friend since we were seven years old; we used to play doctor. Although my profession is not far from Friedman's, I am a doctor, but in another specialty, in another field. I do not know if I could have been a cardiologist, for example, like Dr. Friedman is.

I am happy with my profession. I love psychology. I really like studying and trying to understand what goes on in each human being's head and what drives or motivates them to be who they are. I like knowing that I collaborate with the emotional stability of someone, especially children, who go through so many changes throughout their development, not only those that come from growth but also because their worlds are affected by the people who raise them, who, in turn, bring their own issues.

"Dr. Friedman, my granddaughter Perla, is also a psychologist. She has a clinic for children in Denver, Colorado." Bella said proudly.

"That is great, Perla. Congratulations. Hopefully, one day, we can have coffee and talk about that branch that interests me so much. Hopefully, you will not analyze me and end up sending me to therapy, Friedman said, a little embarrassed and sweet at the same time." I said, and all three of us laughed.

"Call me Salomón, Perla, which is my name, and since we are colleagues, there could be that congeniality between us."

"Until next time, Salomón."

"Goodbye, Perla; see you soon. Isabella, my secretary, will contact you for a follow-up appointment."

As soon as I hung up the video call, Isabella was looking at me with her big eyes without blinking; she wanted me to make some comment. However, we did not have time; the whole family was waiting for us to detail the results of the follow-up appointment with the doctor, although I really had not heard much of what they had talked about; I had no idea what I could say to them, so I improvised.

Aunt Alondra created a group chat a few days ago, to which we were all added. I can see Aunt Alba's name, Aunt Alondra; her husband, Uncle Stefano; Aunt Paloma; also, her husband, Vicente;

Dad, Gabriel, and his wife, Marta; my cousins Peter, Andrew, Mathias, Vicente Jr., Antonio, and, of course, I am Perla. We are all there; only Isabella is missing, who we did not invite to the group because there really is a lot of conflict for her with the cell phone, which she is not interested in now.

After my great improvisation regarding the video call with the doctor, I proceeded to change the subject in a subtle but fast way, inviting everyone to make a group video call so that they could see Bella. That was crazy: Bella and I stood in her dining room, and each entered the family video call from our home. Everyone spoke at the same time, shouted, laughed, and cried, and, even at some point in the conversation, Uncle Vicente forgot that he was not wearing pants, stood up to go to the kitchen, and left his somewhat worn underwear exposed in front of the camera, to everyone's delight. At that moment, we decided to cut the connection to continue it later. There were many emotions together for everyone, especially for Isabella, who, although virtually, could see her entire family gathered at the same time.

At the end of the video call, Bella seemed melancholy, so I decided to invite her to take one of those walks that I had already started in the neighboring golf course, on which Mr. Marlei always accompanied me with his little legs moving at full speed. I already knew which way to go and where to walk to avoid crossing anyone. Isabella agreed very happily. We put on our face masks and grabbed a bottle of water while Mr. Marlei waited for us at the door, jumping with excitement with the leash in his mouth, ready to go out.

Isabella does everything with pauses typical of her age. The walk that for me is always thirty minutes, reaching to walk a little more than two kilometers, today we did it in twenty-five minutes, covering only half a kilometer. We sat three times on different benches around the field; the third time I saw Bella close her eyes and fall asleep for a few minutes, I closed mine, too. As always, I felt her shine by my side; Mr. Marlei even felt her because when I opened my eyes, he was sitting on Bella's feet with his face as if he were looking at the field, but he also had his eyes closed.

I am going to do this more often. I think my grandmother enjoyed it a lot; I could see it on her face. Bella and Mr. Marlei arrived and went straight to sleep for much of the afternoon; they were exhausted. I took the opportunity to call Javier, and while talking to him, a voice message came on my phone; it was from Dad:

Buona notte, *principessa*, I noticed you were a little distracted today. Is everything okay, my love? I just want to remind you that I love you, that I always think of you, and that I appreciate very much that you are with Bella accompanying her. I value your time. Before saying goodbye, I want to repeat that thing that good Gandhi wrote, that you know well that I like to tell you: "Every night, when I go to sleep, I die. And the next morning, when I wake up, I am reborn."

With this, my Gabo reminded me that today stays in today; tomorrow is a different day and will bring a thousand new opportunities. Gabo is always what my heart needs, many times even without me knowing it.

March 25, 2020

"Hi, Jane, darling, it is so good to hear from you, as always."

"Hey Perla, I have been thinking a lot about what we talked about, and it is true: we cannot let the children's therapies fall through. They could be undoing all the progress you and all the psychologists on the clinic staff have achieved so far. I found out early today about an app that allows professional video calls; it has many features that would be useful for us. The video calls can be recorded. It allows using digital whiteboards and adding special sounds, filters, and fun tools for the little ones. I have downloaded it and already started testing it; it is quite interactive. I sent a request to everyone involved to download it. Users called me today, and I gave them passwords for each one. I am excited. I am going to start scheduling appointments with the children's families, but I will call them first to explain everything. You will see that with this, we are going to be able to save the therapies." Jane commented, super excited, almost breathless.

"Oh, Jane, what great news you are giving me; what a magnificent option. It is crazy that we were not even aware of all these technological things; we really need to catch up."

"Yes, yes, although I see a bit difficult the adaptation of the older psychologists to this new way we will propose to attend for now, but you will have to help me with that. Also, I'm thinking of organizing a presentation of the app that is didactic. You could do it. I know you'll convince them quickly; you're very good at that."

"Of course, Jane, whatever you say, I am more than willing."

"Well, dear, I'll leave you now. I've sent you the reports. I have a meeting with the accounting department. We don't know how we're going to manage the rent payment for the clinic's premises in these weeks that we'll have it closed. We're pulling from all sides. I'll tell you later, but first, review the reports. Shall we meet at five? Does that work for you?"

"You are the best, Jane! Thank you!"

This morning, Bella did not get up at six, as she always does. When I went to see her before today's meditation, I found her asleep. I kissed her. She asked me to let her sleep a little longer. I said yes, of course, and continued with the meditation. Then I prepared breakfast. The smell of freshly brewed coffee always motivates her, and today was no exception. When she smelled the coffee, I heard her greeting Mr. Marlei:

"*Buondì*, Mr. Marlei."

Since he came home, Mr. Marlei has decided to sleep at Bella's feet. He does not move from that spot until she greets him, always with a "*buondì*"; at night, it is the same: he takes possession of Bella's bedfoot as soon as he hears she is going to sleep and invites him to accompany her with a *"vai a dormire*, Mr. Marlei." Then, he moves his little legs at full speed to reach Bella's pace; he settles in circles in the bed she ordered for him from Amazon and lies down at her feet.

I heard her wake up, happy like every morning. My soul returned to my body because, for a moment, I thought she felt sick and that something was hurting her. I do not want anything bad to happen to Bella. It saddens me to see her walk slower every day as if she were gradually saying goodbye to life. A few days ago, we talked about that, and she asked me what I would do when this pandemic ends. I told her about my plans with the clinic, about everything we want to grow, and about our desire to continue attending more children. I also told her about getting married and that, of course, she cannot miss my wedding. She smiled, but it was like a smile that disguised something, like something that does not want to be said but is known to be true.

"Perla, dear." She said this later. "Only God knows if I will get to that moment. I am not sure how much time I have left to enjoy you all. I can only say for sure that nothing is eternal, everything is transitory, and everything transforms, so we must be prepared, but mainly understand that we only have this moment for sure."

"Bella, why are you telling me this? If you are not there, I am not getting married."

"Perla, something you must accept about this world is that we are all going to die, some sooner than others. I, for example, am close to that, and we can't deny it but don't worry, dear, I'm not afraid, I'm ready, I've done everything I had to do, I am more than satisfied with my time on this earth, immensely grateful for everything I have been able to live, but above all, proud of what I am leaving as a legacy: you! I just have one pending thing that I am sure we will resolve soon with your arrival."

"Bella, but wait for me a little bit; I still must organize some things. Please be next to me at my wedding." I asked, trying to hold back tears.

"My girl, my Perla, I have had so much love for you always, the long-awaited granddaughter who gave life to my Gabo, the only son I could have. Something tells me that I will not be able to attend your wedding because I also sense that that wedding is not as close as you think. Now let us have that coffee, which smells delicious and is getting cold, and you know well that cold coffee is not my thing."

She left me speechless. I drank the coffee, ate some toast, and accompanied Bella while she finished her breakfast. I took Mr. Marlei out to stretch his little legs a bit and returned to read the reports to catch up with work, but I could not stop thinking about what Bella had told me in the morning.

In the afternoon, I checked the app Jane sent. The truth is that many things can be done with it, so I am going to prepare the presentation to encourage everyone in the clinic to continue their appointments and therapies with patients through this means. Jane's initiative is so good; this is going to help us a lot. In fact, I will start by setting an example myself; I will coordinate my first appointments with some children and their families or caregivers.

Many things have crossed my mind after talking with Bella; she has been telling me about some episodes of her life, as she said she would. It is so interesting to talk to my grandmother, although sometimes I lack hours in the day. I thought I would have plenty of time during the pandemic, as many things have been limited, but now it seems like I have less time than ever. I have set myself the goal of dedicating at least an hour a day to talk to Bella about whatever she wants to tell me about her life; I know it will be very enriching for both of us.

II. A Man from the Planet Mercury

March 29, 2020

Mercury is the smallest planet discovered in the solar system so far and the closest to the sun. The surface of Mercury, similar to that of the moon, is a work of art to my eyes every time I gaze at the images I can find. This is due to the numerous craters caused by meteorite impacts, which give it that asymmetrical imperfection that makes it, in my opinion, more approachable and real. Although the temperatures on this planet are extremely high, more detailed research shows the presence of ice in several of its craters.

On Mercury, there is a phenomenon that leaves me breathless: the phenomenon of double sunrises. When the sun rises, it appears about two-thirds of its size, stops, hides again exactly where it rose, and then reappears to continue its journey across the sky. What a marvel! This phenomenon has captivated me ever since I read about its existence.

As a final note, some research dares to claim that there might have been life on Mercury, given the presence of water in some parts of this planet.

I am not an astrologer, scientist, astronaut, or engineer, but I always liked to toy with the idea that my father, my brilliant Gabriel Martini, is not of this world. This man is simply unique. Today, we talked for an hour without stopping, and I was left with a dry mouth from so much laughter. The topics just flow without pressure or a script. When we converse, we can go from a trivial, frivolous chat to suddenly diving into politics and always ending with very profound topics, sometimes even spiritual, all in the same call and always connecting in a unique way.

"Good morning, princess! How nice to see you on this screen." Gabriel greeted me, drawing a noble smile on his face."

"Are you always this sweet, Dad?"

"Always when I talk to my daughter!"

"Dad, I have been wanting to call you for a long time, but time flies, and I do not know what is happening. Haven't you noticed the same thing lately? I cannot believe it has almost been a month since all this madness started. I will not deny that we are adjusting very well. Bella is wonderful at organizing, and she is always cheerful. Her words are always encouraging; I do not know how she does it."

"Yes, dear, Bella is special; that is why you are the way you are; it is in your veins. But tell me, how is everything going with you, Perla? I mean, what is going through your little head? What is going through your heart? I must confess that I am a bit worried. Whenever you write or we talk, you only tell me about work, Bella, and even Mr. Marlei, but I hear little about your feelings, your thoughts." My dad said, visibly worried.

"How well do you know me, Dad? The truth is, I am a bit confused about my relationship with Javier. I have not mentioned it to anyone, but it is like most of the time I do not feel like I miss him. I realized that all this time I've been living here, I think little about him. I even feel better than ever. I don't think I've felt this good in a long time, and I wonder what will happen when I go back to my life with him or, worse yet, if I want to return to a life with him."

"Perla, in your pockets only put your own happiness; do not depend on other hearts more than your own, much less make any obligations regarding the feelings of others. The only duty you have is to yourself. If you are well, those who belong to your world will be well."

"Dad, I cannot wait for this to end so I can hug you."

After hanging up the call with Dad, my heart returned to its place as it always does every time I talk to him.

April 1, 2020

- Mexico declares a health emergency and suspends all public and private activities.

- Emergency room visits drop, although deaths increase.
- Colombians around the world are stranded by the pandemic.
- The UN and the UK postpone the Glasgow climate summit due to the coronavirus. Spain is in a state of alarm due to the coronavirus.
- The EU foresees that the virus will resurge in a few weeks.
- The United States is the country with the most coronavirus cases in the world, with a total of 216,721 infected.

We have decided to cancel the newspaper subscriptions that arrive at Bella's house; these are today's headlines. I note them because we won't read them anymore. Enough with the news we hear while preparing breakfast. We are also reducing the time spent watching these news programs. We used to watch them for almost thirty-five minutes; now, it will only be a quarter of an hour. We do not need to fill ourselves with so much information, which in most cases is negative.

In two days, I will complete a month since arriving in Florida, initially just for a visit. So many things have happened this month; I have changed my daily routine and think for the better.

I am still amazed at the human capacity to adapt even to situations that were not planned for; this brings to mind a phrase from Viktor Frankl's book that I like so much, Man's Search for Meaning: "When we are no longer able to change a situation, we are challenged to change ourselves."

Today, I started talking with Bella about her life, and I was astonished to learn some further details. Bella, at times, seems not to remember some things; other times, she does not want to think about them again. In our first conversation, we only talked about Gabo, as she knows well that this topic fascinates me. I asked her for permission to take notes, telling her that I wanted to include her memories in this writing; she said she felt flattered.

I think then that we should begin to recount some of what we talked about. I should first provide a few lines about who Gabriel Martini is; I will leave that for tomorrow.

April 2, 2020

I never know where to start when I talk or write about my father or my Gabo, as I like to call him. I think I already mentioned that Bella chose that name for him in gratitude for God's response to her many prayers for a son.

Gabo married my mother deeply in love; he always told me that he loved absolutely everything about her. They met at the office, both working for an important fashion magazine at that time. My mother, Dalva, was starting her first internship as a fashion designer, and my father was making his first steps as a communicator. I was born when they were still dating, and after my birth, they decided to get married. Here, I feel obliged to write what Bella repeats all the time:

"Perla, dear, you are the only daughter of my only son, the only granddaughter of the only son in the Martini family."

According to Gabo, when I was born, love multiplied in our home, so a few years later, my parents began the search for a second baby. When I turned seven, my mom gathered us in the living room, and inside a little box, there was a drawing where she had painted a family tree with the names of my two parents, then my name, and next to it was the word "baby." My father was the first to realize what my mom was trying to tell us: she was expecting a baby, and at that time, she was two months pregnant.

Four months later, my mother's labor was premature. I have a vague memory of what happened: running with my father behind the ambulance that was taking my mother to the hospital. I am not truly clear on what happened; I never asked. I just knew later that my mother died due to fate and medical malpractice. Two days later, without even having buried my mother, the baby brother who would have been my younger sibling also died.

The days following that event are just a blank memory; I have no recollection of anything after that. I understand that this was a tool my mind used to block the immense pain that the whole situation caused me, and for now, I will keep it that way, blocked deep in my brain.

After the terrible loss, my father dedicated himself to me; he devoted his soul to accompanying me in the process of overcoming those tragic events. From day one until today, he has done his work with me impeccably.

On his part, to mitigate his pain, my Gabo sought refuge in spirituality. He worked hard to get closer to his faith and found peace amidst so much darkness, and it was precisely that peace that he transmitted to me. He also gave me strength every time my spirits faltered for a thousand and one reasons; as can be understood, after such an event at such an early age, I was left quite affected.

Not everything was rosy for my father at times, as I often saw him crying bitterly until dawn. In those moments, I would sit behind his bedroom door, looking through the crack, and wonder what he might be thinking. I could only count the minutes waiting for him to stop crying. During many of those nights, those minutes turned into hours, and on some occasions, I saw the morning light coming through the window as he shed his last tears. Among tears, I heard complaints, laments, and reproaches for whoever or whatever had taken his wife and son from him, leaving him alone with the responsibility of a daughter who had been left orphaned and deeply affected by the same event.

Despite everything, Gabo knew how to be chicken soup for my heart in rehabilitation; his love, his company, and his care were always my shield for life.

Almost eleven months after the loss of my mother and baby brother, we received a call from the lawyer handling the case regarding the malpractice that ended my mother's and the baby's lives. He told us that they had ruled in our favor in the final instance and that we had won a considerable amount of money. My father arranged for the money to stay in an account until I was of legal age so that I could decide what to do with it. I used the money at twenty-six when I finished my psychology degree. With the accumulated funds, I made my contribution to the investors and founders of what is now the mental health clinic for children we have in Colorado.

I remember when I called Gabo to ask if he thought it was right to withdraw the money from the bank after so long to invest it in this clinic with other doctors who shared the same dream of creating it. My father replied, "Princess, that money is yours; nothing we do will ever bring back what we lost. However, using it for such a noble cause as allowing thousands of children to have access to mental health, and even, as you tell me, many of these therapies being subsidized by you, is more than a blessing. Your mom, your baby brother, and I are proud of who you are. I trust in your ability as a professional, but above all, I believe in the quality of human being that you are, in the values with which you have been raised until today, and I know you still have much more to give to this world, my dear Perla. Your mother chose your name with so much care; she searched long before choosing it. She knew of my love for the sea, but she also felt that what she was carrying in her womb was a little person who would be unique, who would bring us so much joy, and she was not wrong."

Gabo, with his thick, large but soft hands, when he caresses me, they feel like fine feathers. He has almond-shaped, honey-colored eyes that always light up; his voice is deep but so sweet that every time I hear his voice, it is like a lighthouse guiding me in the infinite sea towards solid ground.

It is not just because he is my father, but I inherited many things from him regarding my physical appearance. For example, the honey-colored eyes—only mine still lack that way of lighting up that Gabo's have.

He loves melodies, which is why there is always good music in his house. He delights in classical works, playing them on his spectacular grand piano, which he diligently cleans every Saturday. But he also enjoys lively salsa, good tropical cumbia, or sensual tango; he enjoys the chords of music regardless of its origin.

After graduating, almost reaching twenty-seven years old, when I was in all the preparations for the official opening of the clinic, Gabo invited me to lunch and asked me to choose the restaurant. Naturally, I chose an Italian one that I love located in downtown Denver, on one of the main streets, where the atmosphere is charming and the food is perfect.

He arrived from the airport directly at the restaurant. I was dying of curiosity to know what he wanted to talk about; for a moment, I thought it would be to congratulate me on the start of the clinic's operations, but I was far from the right answer.

I arrived very punctually, as is my habit, but Dad, as is also his habit, was already waiting for me at the table, having ordered water and white wine for both of us. I was dressed in casual office clothes. It was Friday, and on Fridays, I try to go a bit more relaxed to the clinic, although I never lose my formality. He, on the other hand, looked classic without ceasing to be elegant, as he always does. He had a pristine white shirt and dark blue chinos, was perfectly groomed, and was impeccable in his entire presentation. I wondered how one manages to travel so long on a plane and arrive perfectly for lunch; he has that secret well kept. We greeted each other with a long hug followed by more or less thirteen kisses. We had missed each other a lot; it had been at least eight months since I last saw him.

Gabo told me, without much preamble, that the meeting was to tell me that he had been seeing someone for about a year. He had not told me before because he did not want to distract me from my plans with the clinic; besides, he wanted to be clear about everything between them before telling me.

A good woman. It was the first time he spoke to me about a woman other than my mother. He got emotional and cried as he told me about her, her family, her daughters, and how good it was to be with her. I cried, too. How could I not be happy if the person who until then had dedicated his days and nights to me now found someone to share his moments with and started writing new chapters in his story with that special someone? I was overly excited that he allowed me to be part of it, knowing that Dad would now have someone else by his side.

Weeks later, I met her and was able to confirm all the beautiful things my father had said about her. Marta, as my father's now wife is called, is a beautiful woman on the outside. But especially on the inside, she is cheerful, with a discreet but very cordial smile, educated, always attentive, and willing to help. She also enjoys music very much, like Gabo. They both have many things in common, such as their love for the sea, so they go sailing together, take their books, and spend the entire day between the breeze and the pages of their favorite authors.

They got married the year after the lunch we had that afternoon in Denver. The wedding was in Cartagena, Colombia, where Marta and her family are from. It was a beautiful wedding, full of color, a display of love, culture, and music. They rented a large house on one of the Rosario Islands. We all left wanting to get married; it was a dream.

During their honeymoon, they traveled through many towns in Colombia. Gabo and Marta bought a house in Cartagena, where they now spend half the year surrounded by pleasant weather, friendly people who love them, healthy food, and the sea they adore. The other half of the year, they return to the United States to visit family and share their love. When they are here, they divide their time between Bella's house, my house, and the aunts' houses. Everyone fights to have them in their home; they are pure joy.

How can I not doubt if Gabo is from another planet? He must be a Mercurian; such a special person as he is, I find it hard to believe he is from this world.

April 3, 2020

Writing about Dad in these pages yesterday left me longing to hear his voice again. I waited for a decent hour and dialed his number after my morning meditation and breakfast with Bella.

"Good morning, Mr. Dad."

"Good morning, Princess! Is there a particular reason for this early call? Because I was about to call you, I have some news. Since we managed to get tickets to travel to Florida next week, we have rented a house for four months near Bella's place. It is a big house with several rooms. Aunt Paloma and Vicente are coming too. As soon as we arrive, we will get tested for coronavirus, and we are going to do the recommended ten-day quarantine at home; after that, we will rush to see you. If you want, you can come and stay with us for a few days. The place is beautiful; it is a seven-minute walk to the beach, and there is plenty of space in the house for you. I know Bella does not like to leave her house, even for a night, but we can talk about it. If not, at least we will be closer."

"Gabo, what wonderful news! Thank you for brightening my day like this."

"Yes, Princess, we will see each other soon. I am so excited to see you and Mom. Things are not great here in Cartagena; there are increasingly COVID-19-related deaths, and people are going crazy with the confinement. The situation is tough for many people since they cannot earn money without going out to work. The lady who helps us at home has not been able to come for three weeks because her husband got sick with COVID-19. He is recovering now, but it left him with severe aftereffects, and he is not well. We are deeply sorry for her. We are still paying her; we will not abandon her, but the situation at her home is hard. Her children cannot work as taxi drivers like they used to before the pandemic. You can imagine that there are many cases like hers in the country. There is no end date for this situation; we are all waiting for vaccines to mitigate what is happening."

"Dad, it is heartbreaking what is happening in the world; we are not doing so badly here. At least we have work, and we get state aid. The government has issued economic bonuses for the neediest families. They distribute food at many points in the country for people going through hardships, and there are many places with laboratories set up in parks and pharmacies where people can get quick tests for free to see if they are infected. We are in a blessed country, but I am aware that there are many other places in the world where people have to choose between going out to work to eat and risking getting sick or staying home without coronavirus but starving."

The conversation filled me with hope, knowing I would soon see Dad and Marta, hug them again, and be closer, supporting each other through these tough times for everyone.

Later, we received a call from the hospital where they had taken Bella's neighbor, Mrs. Dorothy, after the accident. They told us what we had been expecting: Dorothy could not survive. In the hospital, she contracted COVID-19, which, combined with the effects of the fall, was too much for her body. Though to me, it seemed like Mrs. Dorothy, knowing her partner was no longer waiting for her at home, let herself go. No force keeps a person alive more than knowing love is waiting somewhere and having the hope of returning to it. There was no wake, no funeral; her family could not see her because of the pandemic—such events were prohibited. The same happened with her husband. Mrs. Dorothy was cremated and then taken to the cemetery to be buried above her husband's grave. The epitaph read: "In our favorite place, the eternal summer, and of course, together."

April 7, 2020

I talked to Javier, but I did not want to mention that Dad and Marta are coming tomorrow; I was afraid he would say he wanted to see us too and that it would cause a fight. Lately, we have been arguing about everything, even more than usual, because he thinks very differently from me. He complains that he does not understand why I have not started looking for a way to leave my grandmother's house. Unlike me, he has only spoken to his father twice since the pandemic began, and only about business; he has called his mother just once, and that was only because she insisted. If it were up to Javier, he would not have called her at all. I, on the other hand, am counting the minutes to see my Gabo.

Isabella is just as excited as I am. We have been preparing since yesterday for what we will eat when the family comes to her house; Aunt Paloma and Uncle Vicente will also come. I do not know how we will all fit in because the apartment is small, but we will manage. Mr. Marlei will surely be scared—he is afraid of everything, though lately, he seems less fearful. He looks braver; he even dared to bark at a dog the other day while we were walking. Of course, the other dog was quite far away; so far it did not even hear him, but I was surprised to see that bravery in him, so I kissed him out of excitement.

"Hi, Perla, I am calling to apologize. I am sorry I got upset this morning when we talked, but I just do not understand you."

"Hi Javier, do not worry. I guess it is because of this strange situation for everyone."

"What happens is that I miss you a lot, Perla. We cannot go on like this; you need to tell your family to take care of your grandmother. You are missing living your life to care for someone who is already on her way out of this world. Besides, you are falling behind in your personal life. You could be here overseeing the clinic's progress. Who knows, they are even stealing from you. How can you trust Jane so much? I do not like that girl much, and you know it."

"Javier, how can you say I am wasting my time with Bella? You have no idea what you are talking about. For me, there is no one on this earth wiser to learn from than her. You know how much I love and respect her. We have talked a lot about Jane, how much I value her, and what an excellent person she is, both personally and professionally. I still do not understand why you keep talking about her like that. You have never even taken the time to get to know her a little. You know she is my best friend, and I have known her since we were kids. We have shared many moments together; you do not value that when you talk about Jane."

"Perla, let us not start. I called to apologize. Don't you see that nothing I say is right for you? I am always the bad guy; you are never happy with anything."

"Maybe you are right, Javier. It is just that these days are very hectic; work is quite intense. We are using that app I told you about for virtual appointments with patients; it is excellent. I am making great progress with the kids' therapies. The families and the kids themselves have adapted perfectly. I am happy with this. Hello? Javier, are you there?"

"Love, I will call you later... I have something more important to do. You can tell me whatever you want later. Kisses, goodbye."

April 18, 2020

Today is my thirtieth birthday. It seems like Gabo planned everything perfectly; his arrival last week was timed exactly right to get the COVID-19 tests, wait for the results, and do the recommended quarantine days.

Everyone came early in the morning with breakfast. Dad, Marta, Aunt Paloma, Uncle Vicente, and Vicente Jr. arrived. The latter was a total surprise, as I did not know my cousin would be staying at the rented house with Dad. When they knocked on the door, I was not even brushed. They pushed the door open and shouted, "Surprise!" Bella, Mr. Marlei, and I almost died from the mix of emotions; we were disoriented but incredibly happy.

From around seven in the morning until five minutes ago, almost eight at night, we have not stopped talking, sharing stories, and recounting all this time we have not seen each other, which, combined with this month of the pandemic, has been a lot. We have realized that we cannot let so much time pass this way again. The last time I saw Vicente Jr., my little cousin, was at Dad's wedding in Cartagena. I was twenty-seven and a few pounds lighter, and he was fourteen, wearing colored braces and thick glasses. Today, instead of that boy came a tall young man with perfect teeth, tousled hair, and a high school heartthrob look. My Gabo was just the same as always, impeccable from head to toe, smelling wonderful with that scent that always accompanies him and lingers everywhere when he leaves—a mix of wood and sweetness, a sensation of oak honey, which is how I always remember him.

At noon, Jane called. We made a video call so she could see my dad, and they talked for a while. Dad cares a lot for Jane. We have lovely memories together from outings, the movies, the beach, and even visits to some of my aunts' houses and some summers with Bella. Jane sent me a gift by mail that arrived yesterday, but she asked me not to open it until my birthday, so I opened it at dinner along with the other gifts. I loved it: it was the latest novel by my favorite writer; this book will keep me company for the next few nights at Bella's house.

On the other hand, my father gave me a beautiful handmade bag from Colombia. He knows I love those things. I appreciate anything handmade, especially from other countries, because it tells the story of the place. Sometimes, I can even smell the person who created the piece; it helps me imagine additional details. Moreover, I know Gabo is like me. He thinks a lot before giving someone a gift, which makes it even more special because it is not just the object itself but also the intangible, the time he took to find it, which for me is a precious asset.

I waited for Javier's call, but he forgot it was my birthday. He has a bad memory and does not organize himself for important dates, and I am always the one keeping track of him. When Dad asked if I had talked to Javier, I tried to hide it, but he noticed; he told me not to worry about explaining then, that we would talk about it later, and that today we would just have a wonderful time.

Bella had somehow ordered a lemon pie from my favorite bakery. It arrived just in time for dessert. As always, my grandmother left me speechless. I have no idea how she managed to order it without me suspecting anything, but she did. Naturally, we all loved it and ate double; by now, extra pounds at home are in abundance during the pandemic.

My grandmother also gave me another gift, a bit mysterious. She gave me a blue box with a small ribbon that made it a bit difficult to peek inside without breaking it. She asked me to open it before bed when I was alone, so I did, and I kept it in the room until everyone left. When I got to the room, quite intrigued, trying to imagine what was inside that box, I went straight to it and opened it. I could not believe what I was seeing! It was Bella's diary! It dates back to the time her grandparents died, which roughly coincides with her first marriage.

I have spent several minutes turning over the idea of whether to start reading it or not; I think before reading it, I must talk to Bella about what I am going to find in case there is something I should know beforehand. In this month that I have spent living with Bella, we have talked a lot about diverse topics. When I ask her about the years she lived outside Florida, mainly the years she lived in Peru before moving to this country, I find some inconsistencies in her story. Something about the topic worries her, which is why I do not insist much; I do not know if it is because she does not remember some things from that time due to her advanced age or because she simply does not want to remember anymore. The diary is beautiful. It is a somewhat faded sky-blue notebook that time has yellowed, and it is quite thick. It looks like it has about three hundred pages, something a bit unusual for a notebook from that time. On the first page, she wrote in cursive:

March 3, 1952

My Diary

BELLA MARTINI

III. The Women of My Life

April 20, 2020

It has been two days since Bella gave me her diary. I have not been able to talk to her much about it. When I try to bring up the subject, she responds that I should finish reading it first so we can discuss it with that foundation.

On the other hand, these two days have been full of events, all at the same time, and they have left me exhausted.

We started with Javier's unexpected desire to come to Florida to spend a weekend with me. He has not confirmed the dates yet, but he is working on it. I think he wants to come partly to mitigate the guilt he felt when he realized he had forgotten my birthday. Upon finding out through a post by Jane on her social media the day after my birthday, he probably almost had a heart attack; he then decided to give me his presence for a weekend, but given the current travel situation due to COVID-19, I don't think he can come as soon as he thinks.

Dad, his wife, my aunt, and her family are very well settled in the rented house. They have arranged for all the groceries to be delivered door to door, so they do not have to go out much and avoid getting infected. There is a protocol for everything, even bringing the groceries into the house. I explained to them the other day how we do it here with Bella, and they liked it a lot, so they are applying it, too. They take turns preparing meals, as everyone in that house cooks spectacularly, and I have heard that even Vicente Jr. knows how to cook very well. They bring the dinner they prepare every day to my grandmother's house, and we here prepare the dessert to accompany the evening. Bella takes great care in presenting a beautiful table with the best decorations, dishes, and fresh flowers. I help her with all this preparation while we listen to some music, always watched by Mr. Marlei's round eyes, following us wherever we go.

For now, Bella's diary reminds me of what I already knew about my grandmother but maybe had slightly forgotten. She started writing it the year her grandparents passed away. I have noticed a strange coincidence between the dates in the diary and what I am currently writing; for example, the diary starts on March 3, exactly the same day I arrived in Florida to see Bella, with sixty-eight years between the two dates.

In these two days of reading the diary, I have gone through moments in my grandmother's life where I could feel traces of melancholy in her early lines, I imagine, due to the loss of her grandparents, who were with her all the time during her childhood and adolescence.

I am delighted with Bella's ability to write so beautifully, even the details of her feelings; the writing of her pages makes me feel as if I were present in the moments she describes. She has dedicated several pages to recounting the relationship she had with her mother. According to her, she did not need any friends while her mother was alive; she filled her days. I will not deny that I have teared up a bit reading about Bella's mother while fantasizing about the idea that I could have had that same close relationship with my mother if she had not passed away.

But not everything was sorrowful in the early pages. Bella writes about her marriage, how she met her first husband, and even gives details of the wedding. In other pages, she talks about Aunt Alba's birth and writes various other details of happy moments in her life. I particularly remember a passage from the diary that caught my attention due to the mixture of feelings Bella expressed, feelings I wouldn't have imagined in my grandmother, not because I don't believe she has the capacity to feel that way, but because being my grandmother, I forget that she was also a young woman starting to discover the world.

* * *

April 10, 1952

I am feeling something increasingly strong for Raúl. I am not sure if this is right, as according to the teachings of the nuns, a young lady should not feel these things, but my heart tells me that I am on the right path and that I should not be afraid to let my love grow.

When Raúl visits me, we always look for any excuse to leave the house and be alone. I remember that in school, the teachers always taught us that young ladies should not be alone with their boyfriends without supervision, but some things are changing these days. My friends tell me that they have even gone dancing with their boyfriends without additional company, and they say I am quite behind the times.

I have discussed it with my mother, but she believes that the right thing is for Raúl's visits to be at home; she always repeats to me that if he loves me, he will respect my parents' rules. So far, I do not see my boyfriend objecting to visiting at home; on the contrary, I think it is more me who would like to be somewhere else with him to get to know him better. For some reason, I feel that at home, he is not entirely free to express himself. It is always at my insistence that we end up going out or doing something that takes us as far as possible from my parents' sight. I find it very pleasant when we are alone and when he kisses me, caresses my face with his hands, and ends up hugging me; it leaves me dreaming, anticipating what will happen in our next meeting.

Raúl is a military officer in the Peruvian army. As he is an orphan, he was raised by his uncles, who encouraged him to enlist in the military service after finishing school. I remember when we met, I was leaving a New Year's Eve party at the Regatas Unión club, which I had attended wearing a beautiful yellow dress that caught the attention of all the girls that night. My mother had bought it from a friend who had returned from Argentina days before with some dresses to offer for sale to her friends. Raúl says he fell in love with me from the first moment he saw me when I crossed paths with him by chance as he was leaving the same party.

"It is not possible that we were at the same party all night. How could I have been so foolish not to see the most beautiful woman in all of Lima in the same hall as me?" Raúl commented as I was on my way out of the club. Then he offered to accompany my friends and me to wait for the transportation that would take us all home."

Since that night, we have not stopped seeing each other. Shortly after meeting, he asked my parents for permission to be my boyfriend. My mother, to whom I had already told everything in detail about Raúl, agreed to let him court me; my father, on his side, thought about it for a few minutes. However, with a glance, my mother, my grandmother, and I urged him to accept the proposal without much hesitation.

My boyfriend is a gentleman, very polite, and chivalrous. I love it when he comes to visit me in uniform. I feel he is so brave. When we are together, everything is joy between us. We are about to celebrate a little over four months of being together. He has helped me overcome the loss of my beloved grandparents, whom I miss so much. Raúl, with his patience, his affection, and his smile, accompanies me at this moment when I need someone special by my side. As my mother says, "Things always happen at the perfect time."

I am sure it was God who sent Raúl into my life. Only someone as heavenly as Him could have found such a perfect match for me and sent him months before what I believe has been the greatest pain I have felt in my life—the departure of my grandparents.

May 1, 1952

What had to happen happened: several days ago, I decided to lie with Raúl. Today, we had planned to go to dinner, and, thanks to my insistence, Mom let us go out alone. Of course, I had to lie and tell her that two couples of friends would be waiting for us at the restaurant. Raúl came to my house around five in the afternoon. I asked my mother to help me with my hair. I wanted to try a new hairstyle I saw in a magazine from Carla, my friend. It took me almost three hours to get ready between the hair, the clothes, and other details.

I do not know if I had actually planned everything without being aware of it or if it just happened casually. I suppose in the end, it was a bit of both, but I do not regret anything that is happening between us.

"Isabella, you look beautiful as always," Raúl said to me when he picked me up, almost whispering."

"And what about you? You are not far behind; you look very handsome too, as always, Raúl."

"Bella, I have a small inconvenience. I have left at home a book that I need to give to a friend before dinner. If you do not mind, we can stop by to get it and then continue with our plans."

"Of course, my love, I do not mind anything that allows me to spend more time with you."

When we arrived at Raúl's house, I noticed his uncles were not there. When I asked him about them, he told me that they had gone to greet a relative who was celebrating a birthday. It was then that it crossed my mind that maybe we could enjoy a moment alone in his house, so I asked him to show me his room. I noticed a small shadow of doubt on his face, but despite that, he agreed.

Raúl's room was quite spacious, perfectly clean and tidy, and smelled of lavender, one of my favorite scents. The room, with a high ceiling, had a large window overlooking the main courtyard of the house. The bed was dressed in blue with golden touches, and on the nightstand, there was a beautiful photo of Raúl that I guess was taken when he was about four years old. It made me feel tender.

Raúl hurriedly took the book, thinking that we would be late for dinner, the same dinner for which, because of what would happen next, we would not arrive. What happened between Raúl and me that night was magical; I had never felt my boyfriend as close as I did that night. I believe we not only gave our bodies but also connected our souls forever. Now, I carry a piece of his soul with me wherever I go. If heaven is as they have told me, I am sure that we visited heaven together that night. Although a part of my mind has installed a sense of guilt that tells me I should not have done or felt anything, I will never regret what we did. My heart screams that I love him more than ever.

* * *

April 27, 2020

The days pass with a routine that I am falling more in love with. This surprises me, as I never thought I would hear myself say that I am enjoying the routine. I have always been afraid of monotony, thinking it would not let me maximize my potential, that it was limiting, and, above all, boring; however, the routine we now have at home gives me security and peace. I like it very much. I feel at peace, and it has been quite easy for me to get used to everything here. Living with Bella and Mr. Marlei is soothing for my spirit.

I am progressing with Bella's diary. I have gathered details about the moment she found out she was pregnant, how she told her parents, how Raúl took it, and even the decision to get married and the early days of their marriage before the baby arrived.

Bella dedicates several pages to talking about Aunt Alba, her first daughter with Raúl. I am delighted to read about the way my grandmother describes the love they both had for baby Alba, how they eagerly took care of her, pampered her, and attended to every detail she needed. With the same dedication, Alba was cared for by her grandparents, Agostina and Antonio, who also gifted Bella a beautiful small house to live in with her husband when they got married. Bella's parents had bought the house some time ago but kept it rented out, waiting for the moment Bella would become independent. Raúl's uncles helped decorate the home, gifting the couple the living room furniture as well as the bedroom furniture for both the spouses and the new baby. Alba was the greatest joy of that year for both families.

I have decided that in the coming days, I will write a little about Aunt Alba, what she means to me, and who she is currently—the woman who, as a child, would bring back smiles to the Martinis after the sudden and painful loss of the grandparents.

Changing the topic a bit from Bella's diary, Javier has confirmed that he managed to buy his ticket. He arrives next week and will be in Florida from Thursday to Sunday. He asks me to stay with him during those days. The idea worries me, especially because of Bella and Mr. Marlei, as they have become so accustomed to me that I cannot leave them alone for so many days. I spoke with Dad, and he wants to take them to the rented house, saying that a trip would do them good. I hope Bella agrees without much fuss; otherwise, I will be very worried.

I talked to Javier about the importance of getting tested before traveling—at least two tests to be very sure he will not bring any illness, especially for Bella. He thinks I am exaggerating, but I do not think so. I will be very attentive to ensure he does what I asked so that we do not face unwanted and unneeded health issues later.

Additionally, today, we spoke with Dr. Friedman, or rather, Salomón, as he has asked me to call him. The appointment was once again via video call, and this time, I noticed Bella was more familiar with the computer. She navigated the screen naturally and expressed herself calmly, without the previous concern of whether she was being seen or heard correctly.

The doctor commented that he saw her very well, as always, even daring to say that he saw her better than the last time. The conversation was quick but very motivating for Bella, who, every time she talks to her doctors, feels renewed as if just seeing them and hearing them say that she looks very well takes several years off her.

Salomón mentioned that they have been reopening the offices for some specialized tests and that he hopes to schedule a physical consultation for Bella in May. He would like to conduct some tests in the office. We will be waiting for the secretary's call to schedule the appointment.

April 29, 2020

My Aunt Alba was born on February 23, 1953, in Lima, the capital of Peru, where she spent her childhood and adolescence surrounded by her siblings and her mother. For much of her childhood, she was also accompanied by her grandparents, Agostina and Antonio, from whom she keeps sweet memories that she treasures to this day.

A professional ballet dancer, she began her career in Peru before emigrating to the United States with her family. Once settled in New Jersey, she resumed dancing in pointe. Besides her dance courses and artistic performances at the ballet school, in her free time, she taught classes to little girls just starting their careers as ballerinas. With the income she earned from teaching, she paid for her own classes and bought her ballet costumes and shoes.

From an early age, Alba took on the self-imposed role of the responsible older sister, taking care of the money and her younger siblings, as well as being the emotional support for her mother during the times they spent together, as she was always present in all of Bella's life events. This is how they formed that unbreakable bond that still connects them today, to the point where they can feel each other in different situations, like when Bella felt, from across the country, that Alba was having contractions to give birth to her first baby. Bella, as everyone remembers, said, "Today my first grandchild is being born; it's today before noon."

Aunt Alba is tall for a ballerina, with extraordinarily long legs, delicate arms, small eyes, and short hair. She says that because of the many buns she wore throughout her life, her hair became very damaged, and that is why she prefers to keep it short to avoid worrying about it.

Alba is the mother of two boys: Andrew, the eldest of Bella's grandchildren, who is thirty-four years old, and Peter, who is thirty-two; both professionals who combined their knowledge to form a renowned law firm in Los Angeles dedicated to immigration cases. They are Aunt Alba's pride, who today, at sixty-seven years old, lives near them, hoping that they will get married one day so she can move close to Bella and enjoy her retirement and her mother's company. These days, Alba is spending the pandemic with Andrew, who has a beautiful house near Malibu, Santa Monica, in California; this allows them to occasionally take walks on the beach, breathe fresh air, and relax together while waiting, like everyone else, for the pandemic to end quickly.

However, Aunt Alba's story has not always been as beautiful as it is today. She met Ray, the father of her children, at nineteen, the same month she arrived in the United States. At that time, they were both the same age. Ray would be my aunt's first and only love.

A few months after they started dating, he decided to enlist in the army because his family could not afford to pay for his college education. He was in the army for three years, during which he only saw Alba when he returned on leave for two weeks every six months, mainly for summer and Christmas.

After completing the three years, he returned from the army and proposed to her. They got married a few months later in a simple wedding attended only by a few family members, as the news and the wedding date caught everyone by surprise. Of course,

Bella was present on that important day for Alba, but for reasons that we all understood later, my grandmother did not like the idea of her daughter wanting to marry Ray at all. However, she knew she could not oppose it, as they were both of legal age. Besides, Bella always repeated to us, as a guiding philosophy for her life, part of Khalil Gibran's poem: "Your children are not your children. They are the children of Life's longing for itself." Therefore, she had to let Alba live her own experiences, even if they eventually caused pain and tears.

Ray turned out to be a jealous, obsessive, and controlling husband who, over time, began to abuse alcohol, which accentuated his explosive character. All this, combined with the birth of the children, brought sadness to Aunt Alba's home, which we didn't learn about until many years later when the boys were already teenagers.

When Alba's children started noticing their father's behavior towards their mother, they took on the role of protecting her during Ray's outbursts, which unleashed their father's anger as they prevented him from carrying out his violent acts against Alba.

Today, recounting all this seems incredible to me, given that Aunt Alba always gave us a smile, a kind word, a gesture of tenderness whenever she could, so we could never have suspected the hell she was living at home, enduring all that for many years.

One time, when the children were eleven and thirteen years old, they went on a school trip that would take the entire day, not knowing what would happen at home with their parents that day. I will not write details of what happened; I can only summarize that on that day, we all found out what Alba had been living through in her marriage for so many years.

We are grateful to heaven that during those days, Aunt Paloma was visiting New Jersey and stayed near Alba's house. It was Paloma who, after calling several times to her sister's house without receiving an answer, decided to go to the door and force her way in, as it was locked and no one came to open it. The scene she witnessed was hard for her to overcome and for all of us after she told us what happened. When she entered, she found her sister unconscious on the floor, lifted her with the delicacy like one lift of a wounded rose, and took her to her car to drive to the hospital, where her life was miraculously saved. Although more than a miracle, we always say it was her strength, the love for her children, for life, and the duty she still had towards her mother that brought her back from death that day.

Aunt Alba's physical recovery in the hospital took almost three months. Isabella moved into her house with Dad to take care of my aunt's children until she could return from the hospital. I remember those three months very well because I also accompanied them. On the other hand, Aunt Alba's emotional recovery would take many more years.

Bella always felt rejected by Ray, which is why she had distanced herself from their home, but during that time, Alba never stopped visiting her mother. Every time she saw her, my grandmother always worried about my aunt's thinness, constantly asking if she was eating well. She also asked her to dress a little better, among other concerns that assailed her at the time, but she found no answer in Alba.

Bella did not need my aunt Alba to speak to understand that something was not right in her home since she married Ray, but she knew she could not do anything if Alba did not want to talk.

Bella regretted for many years after that gray afternoon not having forced Alba to tell her what was happening in her home. In the end, and after a long time, Bella understood that what happened that day had to happen. There was nothing she could have done differently to prevent it, and then she forgave herself for feeling guilty about something she could not have controlled. Similarly, Alba let Ray go and forgot about him.

Today, Alba is synonymous with resilience in the family, our source of water when we are thirsty, the one we turn to for advice in demanding situations. She is love, but above all, forgiveness. Thanks to my dear aunt, today we are even more united and see life differently. We know that Andrew and Peter, my cousins, are the people they are today because their mother managed to transform those terrible chapters of their lives into love, compassion, strength, and inspiration to grow so that today, as immigration lawyers, they can be a light in the tunnel for those people who come to this country seeking to fulfill their dreams but often find nightmares instead.

Ray never tried to contact or even talk to his wife again; in return, she did not press charges against the father of her children. We later learned that it was my father who mediated the situation: he gave money to my cousins' father and asked him to move out of the state, far from them, and finally to sign the divorce papers for my aunt and never contact them again.

Ray complied with this until today. We would later hear my father tell us that occasionally, my cousins call to see if he needs anything. After all, he is a human being, comments Gabo, but Ray never looked them in the eye again. I suppose at least some shame remained with him.

Writing about Aunt Alba's story brings tears to my eyes and a lump to my throat. I am very aware that this is a story many women have gone through, and some are still going through, and at times I think about Javier. I suppose he would not be capable of laying a hand on me, although his way of responding to some situations unsettles me, as he easily loses his temper. I do not know; it is a strange idea that has been going around in my head.

May 4, 2020

I finished packing my suitcase for the weekend with Javier. He arrives in two days, and I have already organized everything. Bella, Dad, and the rest of the family will be at the rented house. I am bringing Mr. Marlei because I do not want to give them the extra task of walking him, feeding him, etc. Besides, in reality, I think I will need those moments when Mr. Marlei and I walk, enjoying a few minutes outdoors; they are always my lifeline during the day. I feel like he knows the exact time because it is precisely then that he comes looking for me with the leash in his mouth, asking to go stretch his little legs, and I take the opportunity to stretch my brain, so to speak, after several hours sitting at the computer working. Mr. Marlei does not know how important that walk together is to me, or maybe he does.

Javier was not happy to hear that I would be taking my new dog, as he calls him, on our "escape," but he had no other choice. I stood firm in saying that I would bring him, and he ended up accepting it. I am packing a separate suitcase with all of Mr. Marlei's things, not just food but also the blanket he always sleeps with, his bed, his favorite stuffed mouse, his dishes, his leash, etc.

"Perla, why do you have that face? Aren't you happy your boyfriend is coming to see you for a few days?" Bella commented.

"Oh, Bella, yes, I am, but…"

"Perla, dear, you do not have to explain. Just think that tomorrow is always bright for everyone, but it will depend on the size of your dreams, the measure of your efforts, and your courage to make that brightness grow or fade. Everything you are today and work to be will undoubtedly bear fruit.

"I know, Bella, but sometimes everything seems strange to me as if I am not the one living this moment; moreover, sometimes I feel that what I do today is not important, that it does not add up for my tomorrow, quite the opposite."

"My Perla, not a single leaf falls from the tree without something in this process transforming after the fall; the tree that lets go of the leaf transforms, the wind that transports it transforms, the ground that receives it transforms, and of course, the leaf transforms." She told me before leaving the room."

I am very ahead with Bella's diary; I am almost halfway through the notebook. I love knowing how happy she was with Raúl and how loved Aunt Alba was. Now I find out how much Bella traveled with her husband throughout Peru since, due to his military career, Raúl was assigned to different army posts in various provinces across the country, even in very remote places that my aunt had to reach with her baby to be with her husband during the time he stayed at that military base.

In those years, trips were mostly made by road and were usually exceedingly long. I cannot imagine making those trips with all the couple's belongings and a young child. They must have been exhausting for Bella, although she does not describe them that way; on the contrary, she always comments on them as a unique adventure that she enjoyed from beginning to end.

Near the end of the day, we made a video call with Aunt Alondra. She is very worried, as well as quite sad, because her only son, my cousin Mathías, 30 years old, is sick, in intensive care because he contracted COVID-19. They have admitted him to the hospital; they live in New York. She told us that the situation of health there is getting worse every day. People are dying on the subway stairs from this disease. My aunt does not understand what happened, how Mathías got infected because they had been careful. Aunt Alondra told us that everything happened in the blink of an eye. It started with a slight sore throat in the morning, and by night, he had body aches accompanied by extremely high fevers. The next morning, he was already struggling to breathe.

Mathi, as we call him in the family, is a very healthy and athletic guy. He does not smoke or drink alcohol, spends his free time swimming, and also likes to run. Those are his favorite sports; he even did them professionally for a long time, but now, due to lack of time, he only does them as a hobby, but he never misses his practices. He meets with his team every week at the club pool he has attended for many years. My cousin is a systems engineer, working remotely from his apartment in Brooklyn since the pandemic started. He lives alone there, my aunt tells us, and apparently, he felt sorry to leave his housekeeper without a job and allow her to continue cleaning his apartment every two weeks. She was the one who came one day with a severe headache, feeling hot and saying she felt body aches from a bad night. However, she had actually been with COVID-19, but since her symptoms were not strong, she ended up passing it off as a simple discomfort. It was that same virus that silently settled into Mathi's home to take him to the hospital in just two days.

Upon hearing this, Gabo told me he immediately called Aunt Alondra:

"Hello, Alondra. We heard about what happened with Mathi from Alba. She called to tell us about the immense pain you are going through at home. We are deeply sorry for all of this. We are united in thought and heart with you, praying for Mathi's health. We know he is a strong boy; we trust that he will soon get through this; we are longing to have him among us with all the joy he always brings us." My father said this, noticeably affected when the call with Aunt Alondra connected.

"Thank you, dear brother. It is what I desire most in this world, Mathías' speedy recovery." Alondra responded with a choked voice.

"Hi, Aunt. We are all here on the phone to give you strength at this moment. Needless to say, how much we love my cousin, we are all very attentive to him." Vicente Jr. added.

"I know, dear. You guys give me much strength. You and my husband are my fortitude at this moment. I take this opportunity to ask you please not to tell Bella about this for now; we do not want to worry her more than she already is about her condition."

"Do not worry, sister. Bella is not aware of anything; that is why we waited for her to go out for a walk with Perla to take Mr.

Marlei before calling you. Rest assured, we can talk without fear of worrying our mother." Gabo confirmed.

"We love you, dear. We will be attentive to your communication. We trust that everything will be fine, that Mathi will soon be back home; it will be so, you will see." Uncle Vicente assured before ending the call.

May 6, 2020

Alondra is currently sixty-two years old. She is Bella's second daughter; the last one she would have with Raúl. A professional accountant, she has always worked in her husband's company. She met Stefano when she was thirty, and two years later, they got married and had what would be the couple's only child: Mathías.

Whenever I talk about Aunt Alondra, I must emphasize her beauty. She has a perfect face, fair skin, and emerald green eyes, and her wavy dark hair makes the perfect contrast with her features, although she is the shortest in the family. However, as I always hear at home about Aunt Alondra, "What she lacks in height, she makes up for in intelligence." She is always one step ahead in everything.

She left home at seventeen with the dream of seeing the world, and that is what she did. She traveled for almost six years across different continents, several countries, various cities, and places from which she always sent postcards or photos to the family so they could see a bit of what her eyes were seeing at that moment. She, always a free spirit, one day met Stefano in New York on one of her return trips after a long trip. He was a couple of years older than her, from an Italian family, and much taller. Besides their dreams of freedom, they shared a passion for traveling.

When Alondra met Stefano, he had a construction company in New York City that he had inherited from his father, who migrated from Italy quite young with his wife and Stefano, who was a baby.

As the relationship with Alondra flourished, Stefano proposed to my aunt that they settle in New York to start planning their future. Additionally, knowing the various skills of his future wife, Stefano offered her a job within his company and a generous share of the profits to motivate her to stay in the family business. She accepted, mainly because she had fallen madly in love with Stefano, as she would later recount, as infatuated as a teenager; what had not happened to her at fifteen happened to her at thirty. "There's no age for falling in love," she would repeat to us every time they told the story of how she and her husband met.

To talk about Alondra and Stefano, one must necessarily mention Mathías, their son. That young man, wherever he goes, wins hearts; it is fun to recall all the anecdotes we have with him and the close friends who have fallen for him in different situations. Besides being handsome, Mathi is a man with a noble heart, and that makes him even more attractive.

He also learned from an early age one of the most important virtues for the Martini family: punctuality. He arrives everywhere, competing with Dad to be the first to show up.

Mathías is the gift that life gave his mother because, when she was young, my aunt Alondra, after an illness in her ovaries, was informed by doctors that she would not be able to have children. However, she never lost hope or gave up.

Alondra, along with her sisters and my grandmother, are the women of my life, the ones who have always accompanied me throughout these thirty years. I have carried their stories with me wherever I have gone, remembering at each stage of my life their advice, which I treasure deep in my heart. Their unconditional support has made my mother's early departure bearable, not only for me but also for my father.

I am Perla Martini, thanks in large part to the women I have introduced in this diary, not to mention that Aunt Paloma's story is still pending. I will tell you about that one later.

IV. Elusive Happiness

May 8, 2020

Many events have happened in such a brief time, but I want to start by writing about my cousin Mathías. Today at noon, Aunt Alba called to tell us that Mathi has responded very well to the treatment. They managed to remove the tubes that kept him breathing in an induced coma, so he is now conscious and breathing on his own, although with difficulty. The doctors have shown positivity in his progress. Aunt Alba told us that one of the nurses helped Aunt Alondra and Uncle Stefano make a video call with their son; although they did not allow Mathi to speak, it was enough for them to see him for a few minutes and know that he could hear them. I am sure that having wonderful people on the other end of the phone, eagerly waiting for us to recover, gives us the push we need in those moments. I would even dare to say that perhaps that call was as healing as the medicine itself. Aunt Alba told us that if Mathi continues to progress as he has, he might be discharged in a week.

The complicated part comes now because we could not contain the news of Mathi's infection and subsequent hospitalization any longer. Bella found out about it last night. At first, she seemed to take it well, understanding that my cousin was starting to recover, but her nerves got the better of her. This morning, Dad found her in bed, unable to get up; she was conscious but without energy, apparently without strength. We contacted Dr. Salomón, who asked us to bring her in for emergency treatment, as she might be suffering from a heart attack.

My father hurried to start the car while Vicente and Aunt Paloma looked for the wheelchair to seat Bella and take her to the hospital. At the same time, Marta searched for my grandmother's purse to get her insurance documents and have them ready. When they arrived, Salomón was waiting for them; he had already made arrangements for Bella's admission. Without wasting time, they found an available room and prepared her for the necessary exams.

No one else could enter the hospital but the patient; for that reason, communication with the doctor was constant, and we were all very worried. Dad stayed at the hospital door and sent everyone else home in the car so they could wait more comfortably. Near the hospital was a café, where Dad could rest while waiting for news from the doctor and trying to think about something else by reading a book.

I found out about Bella's hospitalization tonight while Javier and I were having dinner. In the rush to write all these updates, I have not mentioned that Javier arrived yesterday. I have been busy with him, listening to all the stories he had pending to tell me about mutual friends, people who have been sick with COVID-19, and their recoveries, among other things. Today, when I found out about my grandmother, my spirits obviously dropped, which Javier did not like much.

I talked to my father, and we agreed to meet at the café tomorrow. I want to at least be close to him to give him strength. I am confident that Bella will come through this as she always does, but I do not want my dad to go through this worry alone. Also, it will do me good to go out for a while and see my dad. Javier has assured me that he can take care of walking Mr. Marlei while I am out. He knows I do not like leaving Mr. Marlei alone for so long.

May 9, 2020

I left the house early to meet my dad at the café, as we had agreed. As is my custom, I arrived before the agreed time, so I decided to go ahead and order the coffee with some accompaniments for when Dad arrived. I ordered the Caribbean guava and cheese pastries that he loves so much, two coffees with milk, toast, and butter. When I received the order, I sat down to wait for him.

"Perla? Perla, what are you doing here so early?" Salomón asked, recognizing me in the café."

"Salomón? What a coincidence! Forgive me for not recognizing you earlier; I was distracted thinking about so many things." I replied.

"Do not worry, Perla. I understand. We have never met before; I mean, in person. It has always been by video call."

"That is true; this is actually the first time we met. I am waiting for my father. Last night, I found out about my grandmother. Just these days, I am... " I did not know if I should tell him that Javier was in town and that I was not with Bella when the emergency happened."

"I have good news for you." Salomón interrupted, seeing that I was hesitating."

"Do not worry, I have time. Let me join you at the table to wait for your dad together. It would be an honor for me to meet him."

"Sure, sit down. It would be a great favor if you could tell me about Bella's health. We are all very worried, although Dad told me that he was able to talk to her yesterday, thanks to you."

After a while, Dad arrived. He was surprised to see us sitting at the table. The doctor's face did not seem familiar to him since he had not actually spoken with Salomón face-to-face, only by phone; however, upon hearing his voice, he quickly recognized him.

Indeed, Salomón gave us good news: Bella was stable. The tests they had done were to decide if they could perform the intervention they had pending before the pandemic to clean her arteries and also place a stent in one of them so that the blood would flow better. The test results were positive, so everything was ready for the procedure. The speed took us by surprise, but

Salomón reassured us by explaining exactly how the procedure would be done; he also mentioned that this intervention was an exception given Bella's emergency, as operations were currently suspended.

Without realizing it, time passed very quickly. I had left home before seven in the morning, and it was almost two in the afternoon. Dad and I were still in the café. We had not stopped talking since we sat down, and when we noticed the time, we were surprised.

"Dad, it's late; time has flown by. I do not want to keep you any longer. Salomón has agreed to let us know what time the procedure will be tomorrow. He will also tell us how we can see Bella, even if just for a little while, after the procedure. Now, we just have to wait."

"Yes, dear, it is better that I go home to tell everyone what happened today. I have sent them a message saying everything is in order, so they will not worry, but I am sure they are waiting for details. I think I am going to make a group video call with the family so that everyone is up to date with the latest news. I adore you, princess. I hope you can join the video call tonight; if not, we will talk as soon as you have any news from the doctor." Dad replied in farewell.

After Dad left, I stayed a little longer in the café, trying to process everything that had happened in the last two or three days. Among those thoughts, Salomón's voice crossed my mind; now that I knew him face to face, my curiosity about how he would look dressed without the doctor's coat I always see him in, what he did in his free time, who accompanied him at home, etc., increased.

When I finally stopped daydreaming, it was even later, and I ran to the car to see Javier; I also wanted to know about Mr. Marlei.

Upon arriving at the apartment rented by Javier, I found the door open, and inside, neither Javier nor Mr. Marlei were there. I assumed they had gone for a walk, as he had promised to do. I decided to go to the kitchen to prepare a sandwich for us to eat when they returned. On the way, I found Mr. Marlei's leash on the floor, so they could not have gone for a walk without the leash, and then I ran to get my phone to call Javier.

"Javier! Where are you? Where is Mr. Marlei?"

"Perla, I need you to listen to me. Your dog has escaped from the house. I have been looking for him for over an hour, but I cannot find him. He will surely show up. Do not worry." Javier answered without much evident concern.

"Javier, what are you telling me? Mr. Marlei could not just open the door and go for a walk; he is a small, elderly dog, and the worst part is that he is in a neighborhood he does not know, far from what he recognizes as his home. What did you do?"

"Perla, please! What are you blaming me for? I just went out to pick up the pizza I bought, and when I came back, he was gone, disappeared. How can that be my fault?" He argued angrily.

My heart was pounding intensely, my hands started to sweat, and my anxiety began to surface. I decided to grab my main belongings, put them in my bag, throw everything into my car, and go out to look for Mr. Marlei. While driving, I remembered that at noon, when I walked him, he always wanted to stop to greet a dog that peeked out from behind a gate. They played for several minutes as if they had known each other for years, so I thought Mr. Marlei might have remembered how to get there. I hurried to drive to that place.

I parked my car almost in front of the house and heard barking in the distance coming from inside. It was not just one dog; there were several barking. I could recognize Mr. Marlei's bark, and tears ran down my face. I quickly knocked on the door to ask about my dog. When it opened, Mr. Marlei came running out, wagging his tail, happy. I felt he wanted to tell me that he had been playing with his friend, having a wonderful time, and asking if he could stay a little longer.

Seeing me cry, the lady of the house understood that Mr. Marlei had escaped. She said she found him at her door barking, so she decided to let him in.

"You have a beautiful dog. As soon as I heard him bark, I opened the door for Max to come out and greet him, but I was surprised to see him alone, without you." Carla commented, Max's owner.

"I am so sorry, Mr. Marlei escaped from my boyfriend. I do not know how I felt he was here; I almost died of fright."

"Calm down. Nothing happened. Calm down." She said and handed me a glass of water."

"Your dog is fine. In fact, I have not seen Max play so much in a long time. He is happy with his little friend's visit."

"Thank you, really. I appreciate you opening the door for Mr. Marlei to let him in. Sorry for all this drama, but you do not know what kind of days I have had."

"Do not worry. Seriously, it was nothing. I always believe that people who are on the same wavelength find each other, so we have a duty to help each other. I can see that you love your dog, just as I love mine, and that has united us."

Mr. Marlei and I said goodbye to our new friends to head to Bella's house. That night, the rain was extremely intense, and the sky suddenly darkened and was only illuminated by the lightning of the coming storm. At Bella's house, we would wait for tomorrow. I slept hugging Mr. Marlei to the point that sometimes I felt I was suffocating him, but without complaining, he understood that I needed him very much that night.

May 10, 2020

I woke up early to a call from Salomón.

"Hello, Perla, forgive me. I woke you up."

"Do not worry, Salomón; on the contrary, thank you for calling and for your concern in helping us with this whole situation."

"Perla, I managed to arrange for you to wait in my office while we perform the intervention on Bella. When she comes out, you can see her. What we need is for you to bring a negative result from a rapid COVID-19 test and to comply with all safety regulations regarding the pandemic."

"Of course, do not worry. I will do everything you ask. I will see you at seven-thirty at the hospital entrance. Does that sound good?"

"I think it would be better if we met at seven at the café you already know, so I can have a coffee before going into the hospital."

I started my daily routine, then looked for something to wear to look presentable at the hospital, trying not to seem overdone for the occasion. While brushing my hair, I wondered why I was so concerned about what to wear. I first went to Dad's house to drop off Mr. Marlei before going to the hospital. I did not want to leave him alone all day, especially after what happened yesterday.

"Thanks, Dad, for staying with Mr. Marlei. You know he behaves very well. He will not give you any trouble, but please do not let him go out alone for any reason. Lately, he likes to greet his friends without asking for permission."

"Perla, do not worry about anything. Mr. Marlei is a sweetheart; we all love him very much. By the way, you did not tell me how things went with Javier. He is leaving today, right? What time is his flight? Are you going to say goodbye to him?"

"I have not had time to tell you about that story, Dad; it is a bit long. Maybe when I come back for Mr. Marlei, we can talk about it."

"Of course, dear. I will be waiting for your return to chat a bit. You seem worried. Did you talk to the doctor?"

"Yes, Dad, everything is fine with Bella. She will come out quickly, and as soon as I know she is out, I will call to tell you. I am not worried about that."

"Then it is about Javier! I know we have agreed to talk when you return, but I do not like letting you go, knowing that so many things are going through your head and your heart. You're late, but I just want to remind you, my love, that the people who make our world beautiful are the ones who accompany us on the journey, illuminating our steps; when they take our hand, they make us feel in a safe harbor, and they lend us their shoulder not only to lean on but also to jump from. Let us strive to have people with transparent eyes and sincere smiles who bravely give themselves to be known and, with the same bravery, want to know us. Let us admire the decision of these people to add to our lives and allow us to add to theirs.

You know well that I passionately believe these people exist, that there is one for each of us, but if we lose ourselves in time, plucking daisy petals, it will be difficult to prepare for the moment to meet this person. I always think of you, my dear Perla, always praying for you." Gabo finished, giving me a long hug, which I happily received.

On my way out, I passed by a nearby park where they had set up tents for COVID-19 tests. I found the rapid test section and got tested, which came out negative.

Everything went well at the café with Salomón. We mainly talked about the procedure, how long it would take, and the expectations at the end, and he gave me the steps I needed to follow to enter the hospital.

Bella's intervention went wonderfully, and as we expected, Salomón contacted me as soon as it was over.

"Perla, everything went excellently. Your grandmother is on her way to her room. I still have some patients to visit, but I will see her as soon as I can. For now, wait. I will send you a message with the room number so you can see her. Please remember everything I mentioned about the safety procedures, and when you finish the visit, let me know so I can tell you what to do.

"Thank you, Salomón. I will call my family to tell them while I wait for your confirmation of the room number. Thank you again; you do not know what it means to us what you are doing.

"Do not worry, Perla; it is all from the heart. See you later; I have to go.

I immediately called Dad to give him the good news. He said he would notify the aunts, who had been waiting for my call. While waiting, I could not help but look around Salomón's office. It was quite organized, except for some papers scattered on the desk. I will not deny that I wanted to organize them, but I restrained myself as I did not want Salomón to think I was snooping through his documents. I got stuck looking at the framed photos in his office: there were three, one showing a slightly younger Salomón holding his graduation certificate and another more recent one with older people, who could be his parents. The last one, which I stayed fixated on, was a photo taken apparently at Christmas. It showed a family of about eleven or twelve people, with a teenage Salomón. I estimate he was sixteen or seventeen years old. They were all posing around a decorated table, eating, and behind them was a large Christmas tree with simple but, in my opinion, very tasteful decorations. I was distracted thinking about all the possibilities of that photo when I received a text message from Salomón with my grandmother's room number: "Room 707. Please text me when you are done.

* * *

November 4, 1957

The pain in my chest has not let me breathe all day; every time I try to inhale, it feels like it is breaking, as if a large knife is stabbing me straight in the middle. Mom has died without saying goodbye to me. Yesterday we talked. I saw her, touched her, caressed her, and hugged her. If today I had known that I wouldn't be able to hear her anymore, I would have left everything aside while she spoke. I would have focused on making every word that came out of her mouth my own. I feel like we ran out of time, Agostina; we ran out of time to listen to each other and to love each other. It seems unreal, like a bad dream that, when I finish writing this, you will be there with the tea, as always, calling me to sit and have it together that you would ask me again if I ate, as you always did. Agostina of my life, you have always been my escape from everything. Where am I going to run now, if not to you, where, Mom?

* * *

May 15, 2020

A few days have passed after all the commotion with Bella. I have a couple of things to write about; I think I will start by saying that she is doing very well at home with me and Mr. Marlei. The recovery is good, although she is still in pain, so we try to do everything slowly with her. We have decided that these days, not everyone from the rented house would come together; they come alternately, one day some and the next day others, so there are not too many of us in Bella's apartment, which is small; we do not want to overwhelm her while she recovers.

We are much more careful regarding the safety and cleanliness of everyone who enters the house. Salomón has warned us about the importance of extra precautions due to COVID-19. It would be fatal if Bella got infected at this stage.

"Perla, my friend, how are you? It is so good you called; I had something important to tell you."

"Jane, forgive me; you know how I have been these days with my grandmother's situation, but we are getting through it. Tell me, has something important happened at the clinic? I forgot to sign something, right?"

"No, no, Perla, what I want to tell you is something private, so I asked you to call me in your free time. I needed to talk to you."

"Jane, you are worrying me. Tell me what happened. Are you okay? You look pale; I have noticed it for days. I did not want to mention it to avoid alarming you, but has something happened to you?"

"I am pregnant, Perla. I am going to be a mom; you are going to be an aunt!"

"Jane, my friend, I know how important this news is for you and how much you both have been looking forward to this. I have no doubt that you will be the most beautiful pregnant woman I have ever known, and everything will be fine. You have your husband who adores you, but I am also here for you, always for you, as always and forever."

"I know, Perla, that is why I had to tell you because I wanted to share my happiness with you; you know how special you are to me. I love you, my friend! And do not worry about anything;

everything is fine here, and the clinic is progressing, as you well know. Do not worry about the company; focus your energy on yourself, your grandmother, and your family, who love you. Enjoy them."

After finishing talking with Jane, I received a message from Javier; we had not spoken since the day I left upset with him over what happened with Mr. Marlei. He wrote, "Can we talk?"

I do not want to deal with that right now; I did not reply. I hope to be in a better mood tomorrow to respond. I know I have to talk to him. Maybe I am just postponing, delaying the pending talk with him.

A new puppy has arrived in Bella's neighborhood. Mr. Marlei has become obsessed with visiting him every morning during our first walk of the day. The puppy's name is Ulises, and he is a bit shy. I think Mr. Marlei overwhelms him with so much excitement. He is also small and gray in color. His owner told me she adopted him from a shelter for older dogs where most are there because their previous owners passed away. Ulises is an adult dog, just getting used to his new home and his new family, so he is still timid. Mr. Marlei enjoyed playing with him as much as he could and returned home exhausted.

Last night, I finished reading Bella's diary; I have had many mixed emotions. Bella grew from a young girl in love and discovering life to a woman, a responsible, loving mother, and a worried wife, very attentive to the details of her home. Finally, she ends on the last page of this diary, reliving a very painful moment, such as the departure of her mother. I always knew from stories and from Bella's own words how important Agostina was to her, but in the diary, I could see that over the years, my grandmother synchronized her life with her mother's. They united more each day, so her departure was a hard blow for her.

During the time I have been reading Bella's diary, I have been discussing it with dad, who seems quite interested in everything I tell him about what I am discovering. He confessed that he was not aware of some stories I read or, in any case, did not remember them.

Today, I discussed the end of the diary with Gabo. I read the last page to him, and we both were speechless. I suppose dad remembered how terrible it is to live through the departure of a loved one, as he went through that when my little brother and my mother died; I felt guilty thinking that maybe I should not have mentioned it. I have thought that tomorrow I will talk a bit with Bella about the diary. She asked me today when I think I will finish it. I changed the subject; I wasn't ready to tell her that I finished it because I would inevitably have to say that I felt very sorry for her mother's death and that it touched my soul to read that she had such a hard time. I feel sad thinking that Bella went through that while having a small baby and being pregnant with another.

May 16, 2020

"Good morning, Bella. Sit down. I made coffee with strawberry pancakes, just the way you like it."

"Good morning, dear, but how are you? You still have not told me anything about the diary I gave you. You must have finished it by now, right? I know how much you love to read and how fast you do it."

"Yes, that's true, Bella. I finished reading the diary a couple of nights ago, although I have not wanted to discuss it with you yet; the last page is very intense. Thank you for trusting me with the writing; it has been an honor for me to read it."

"No, Perla, thank you for taking the time to be here with me and for the love you give me every moment you are by my side. Maybe for you, it is a new adventure to spend these days here at home, but for me, it has been life. You gave me an invaluable gift. I want you to know that since you arrived, I have had nothing but joy by your side. I thank you sincerely for all these moments of happiness."

"Bella, do not say that the only one who should be thanking is me for everything you have given me since my childhood; you cannot imagine what you mean to me or how good it feels to be here together. The debt will always be mine; I am just trying, in some way, to repay you a little of what you have always given me."

"I have something for you, dear; on my bed, there is something special that is now yours."

I could not wait a second to be in her room and see what she had left on her bed. I could not believe it; I had a new diary in my hand, one that would be the continuation of the first one I had just finished reading. I stood there, mouth open, trying to glance at the first pages, but I remembered that Bella was waiting for me to finish our coffee together.

After breakfast, I wanted once again to leaf through the new diary I had in my hands. However, my cell phone alarm disagreed, as its sound reminded me that I had an important virtual meeting with the office in Denver in forty-five minutes, and I had to start getting ready. Also, after that, I had to take Mr. Marlei for a walk because today they were coming to bathe him. Once a month, a van from the vet clinic comes where they bathe him and cut his hair very well, although, of course, when Mr. Marlei hears the van's horn, he runs to hide to try to escape the monthly bath, as is fitting for him.

The virtual meeting with the clinic in Colorado was productive. Things are going well, progressing little by little; we managed to create a virtual event to replace the conference we had planned months ago, which was canceled due to the pandemic. Many of the people who were committed to the previous conference have confirmed their participation in this one, and that keeps us quite motivated. Regarding the clinic's rent, we have secured state assistance to cover part of the rent to avoid losing the location, as the facilities can hardly be used for therapies and consultations, making it not very profitable to keep the clinic open; we are even negotiating with the owners of the place for a rent reduction for the next three months. Everything is looking favorable for us in this regard; we hope it continues to be so.

Finally, I gathered the strength to write to Javier. We agreed to talk tomorrow night; it is the best time since we both have free time then. I am not quite sure which direction the conversation will take, but I am thinking of being transparent with him about my doubts and feelings; it seems to me that taking that path is the best way for us to understand each other. Hopefully, we will reach an agreement for the good of our relationship.

V. My beloved Raúl

These days have been quite calm, or at least it seemed so. They went by between routine, Bella's recovery, which is going wonderfully, and an event that has us all excited: we are organizing a birthday dinner for my grandmother, who will turn ninety on June 5th. It will be something intimate, basically among those of us living together these days, and we will do it in the rented house. We will all prepare some of Bella's favorite dishes. My dad thought that we could invite Salomón to the dinner as a thank you for all the love and concern he has shown my grandmother so far. The funny thing is that I was tasked with the invitation. I must do it these days so that we have the response in time. There will only be one more person at the table, but that's how my family is; they like to have everything under control when it comes to organizing a gathering.

I had a long-awaited conversation with Javier. It did not go as I had planned, but I am quite calm.

"Hello, Perla. How have you been? He asked me, though without much interest."

"Hello, Javier. I am very well; thanks for asking. Here, with the clinic stuff, with the therapies, with my grandmother's recovery, among other things."

"It is good that you are well and that everything continues normally for you; the truth is that on my side, it is not the same. Since I returned from Florida, I have not stopped thinking about us, about how distant we are. I have noticed that since you left, you have changed a lot, and I do not like what you are becoming."

"Javier, I am not becoming anyone other than myself. What might be happening is that, yes, it is true, I am changing, but my change is normal and inevitable, like the process of transformation from caterpillar to butterfly. I am in a stage of growth, and I do not think it is something you should be scared of, on the contrary."

"No, Perla, I do not agree with you. You are being selfish as always, only thinking about yourself, not realizing that with this thing you call 'your process,' you are disrupting my peace. I am not willing to sit and wait to see how that happens. I think we should think things over. I want to take some time to meditate on what I really want if I want you to continue being part of my life."

"Are you telling me you want to end the relationship, then?"

"Not to end it, I am telling you we need to take this time. I need to think things over better. Give me a few days to get organized. I ask you to wait for me to contact you when I have clarity because right now, I do not have it."

I started reading Bella's new diary. She began to write it in the first months of 1958 when she was pregnant with Aunt Alondra. Her life revolves around taking care of Alba, the house, her husband Raúl, and the sweet anticipation of Alondra's birth.

* * *

April 13, 1958

Today, my little Alondra was born. She was born perfect, with the ideal weight and measurements. The nurses have fallen in love with her because she is particularly good; she hardly cries, just eats, then sleeps, then eats again, and then sleeps again.

Alba came to meet her this afternoon. She is happy with her little sister and wants to take her home. We laughed at her innocent comments. For now, Alba is being taken care of by dad along with Ana, the girl who helps us at home while I recover from childbirth since Raúl is staying at the hospital with me to help these days, although, to be honest, this birth was much easier than the first. Alondra came out without a fight. The breastfeeding process is also going quite smoothly. The baby latches on well, and that helps me relax so that the milk flows without complication. Having Raúl by my side in all this is especially important; it gives me security. Also, knowing that Alba is at home in the best hands, my father's, takes a huge weight off my shoulders. It is heartwarming to see dad so excited about taking care of his eldest granddaughter.

Alondra's birth came at the perfect time, a few months after we buried mom. After that, dad and I have been quite affected; however, the arrival of my little one has allowed us to clear our minds a bit. I cannot deny that, at times, I think about how amazed mom would have been to meet Alondra; she would have cared for her with as much love as she did with Alba.

Raúl is happy. I even noticed him more involved with Alondra than he was with Alba. I understand that she has found him at a different moment in our lives, perhaps more mature. Alondra's arrival was so sought after by us, whereas with Alba, we were caught off guard, even scared. At that time, everything was a test and trial. Now, we are more aware; it is as if we already know why the baby cries, what hurts her, what she needs, etc. My husband is the best father my princesses could have, definitely. I am so grateful every day for him.

My beloved Raúl, how wonderful life is by your side.

* * *

June 5, 2020

We started the morning rushing between calls to congratulate Bella and preparing dinner to celebrate her ninety years. We have decided it will be a surprise, so we are trying our best to hide what we are doing from her. For now, I told my dad to call a few days before to invite us to spend a few days at his house, so Bella thinks we are going just for that reason. I had been preparing the lasagna since yesterday and left it ready just to pop in the oven at dad's house. Uncle Vicente told me they had prepared chicken with mushrooms in white wine sauce, which turned out very tasty; dad had taken care of the two different salads and also prepared one of Bella's favorite desserts: panna cotta with strawberries.

Marta bought golden balloons on Amazon with the numbers nine and zero for the decoration. Days before, and without Bella noticing, we took tableware from her house to organize the dinner as my grandmother liked. Vicente Jr. made a Zoom group so that those who were far away could see the gathering. They all connected at the agreed time, quietly waited for Bella to enter the house, and we all shouted together:

"Surprise!"

Salomón arrived punctually.

"Thank you for the invitation, Perla. I had a wonderful time. Your family is lovely, just like you. He said with a smile as he left."

"Thank you for coming, Salomón, for taking the time."

"I would not miss your favorite patient's ninetieth birthday for anything. I will not deny that with all this COVID-19 madness, I was a bit scared, but the truth is that all these months without going anywhere have made me quite bored; I cannot wait for life to resume. I hope this does not go on for much longer."

"That is true; we are all wishing the same. I hope you liked the food; we spent several days planning this moment for Bella. She deserves everything."

"The food was excellent; I enjoyed it very much, especially the lasagna. Where did you get everything? I need to order food from that place."

"I made the lasagna myself. I told him, laughing. In fact, we did not buy anything; we made everything ourselves. We know it is the best gift we can give my grandmother. She values homemade food a lot."

"Say no more. You have to give me the recipe for everything. Better yet, you have to teach me yourself to make something that delicious. You do not know the favor you would be doing me. I am basic at cooking, and I am already quite bored of boiled chicken and steamed vegetables. Salomón replied, blushing but very sure of what he was saying."

"Of course, whenever you want, we love cooking at home, and I am no exception."

"Then it is a deal, Perla. You see, I am very formal with my deals."

"And I am also very formal with my deals." I said, smiling.

The dinner was an absolute success. Bella was happy. How could we not celebrate the birthday of this wonderful woman? We surprised her. She had not suspected what we were planning, and hearing everyone's voices shouting "surprise" moved her. She enjoyed every detail we organized. In the end, we sang at the top of our lungs the songs we had recorded in our memory, thanks to my grandmother always playing them while cooking. What a beautiful night! We ended it on a high note, as my cousin Antonio, son of Aunt Paloma and Vicente, is a guitar enthusiast, plays beautifully, and also has a wonderful voice. He performed one of Bella's favorite songs, *"El día que me quieras,"* the original tango version by Carlos Gardel. We all had goosebumps. My cousin has that magic when interpreting songs; he is a prodigious artist, without a doubt.

I go to sleep satisfied. We had a spectacular night full of emotions. Between dad and me, we put Bella to bed, but before saying goodbye to her, we talked a little more in bed, the three of us. Bella told us about her time in Argentina, the times she traveled to that country, and how much she always enjoyed tangos, so every time she visited Buenos Aires, she went to as many theaters as she could to see the shows that were presented. When I hear her stories, I feel present. I feel like I am there; the same happens when I read her diary: on each page, I feel the moment as if I were part of that story.

February 23, 1959

We celebrated the birthday of my precious Alba; today, she turned six years old, bringing joy to our lives. Raúl spared no effort to make his eldest princess's party unforgettable. We dressed the house in pink, which is Alba's favorite color so far. We ordered the cake from Doña Francisca, who, in my opinion, makes the best cakes in Lima. We asked dad to speak with the lady who helps clean his house so she could come early to ours to help us keep everything clean since Ana was in charge of helping us set up the tables with sweet and savory snacks for the guests. We bought the dresses for the girls at a boutique where they made them to measure. They turned out beautiful; they looked like two dolls. Dad stayed late last night, helping with the decoration so it would be ready on time.

Everything turned out wonderfully. The guests enjoyed what we prepared with such excitement. Alba was running and smiling all afternoon at her birthday party. That was our greatest reward; seeing our little one smile as she did today made us happy.

In a few months, Alondra will turn one year old, and we also want to do something special for her. Raúl is excited; he has already started planning some details for the party we are thinking of having in April for the youngest member of the family.

* * *

June 7, 2020

"Hello, Perla, I am sorry to call so early, but I need to tell you something important."

"Hello, Jane, you do not have to apologize. Call me whenever you want; do not worry. But tell me what happened. You sound quite uneasy."

"Perla, I am deeply sorry to be the one to give you this news. I know you were somewhat distant from Javier, but I think you need to know this."

"Jane, please, you are scaring me... Tell me what happened."

"Javier's dad has passed away."

"What? When did it happen? How did it happen? Are you sure about this?

"Yes, Perla, Javier's dad died yesterday afternoon in the hospital. They had taken him urgently to be admitted that same day because he could not breathe. He had contracted COVID-19 three days before, but he did not want to tell Javier. He did not allow his mom to tell anyone. You know how Mr. Javier is; he does not like to feel useless."

"I cannot believe what you are telling me, Jane. I am shocked by the news. I do not know what to do. Do you think I should travel to be with Javier at this moment?"

"Perla, I think the best thing would be to call Javier. Offer him your condolences, and ask him how you can help. He might ask you to come back. Although there is something else that I need to tell you."

"Tell me, Jane, please. Everything you have to say, say it."

"I have run into Javier at the supermarket near my house twice this week, and both times, I saw him with the same girl. The first time, I did not let him see me, but I saw him clearly. He was happy, and they were chatting amiably. The second time, I could not hold back and went to greet him. He was obviously surprised to see me, and I think he did not remember I lived near that place. He greeted me curtly, did not even give the girl time to face me, grabbed her arm, and quickly walked away."

"What are you trying to tell me about this, Jane?"

"I am not trying to say anything, Perla. I am just telling you things as they happened these days. I did not tell you before because I did not think it was important, but now that you are going to call Javier, I wanted you to be aware of this."

The news had me worried all day. I kept thinking about going to be with Javier. I even started looking for tickets to travel to Colorado, but I realized I could not do anything if I did not talk to him first.

"Hey Javier, I heard about your dad today. I am so sorry. I wanted to call to offer my condolences. I am sorry you are going through this."

"Hey, do not worry. I am fine. You should not have bothered calling me. I know you have a busy life in Florida with your family." He said to me sarcastically.

"What?"

"You are asking "what" to me? That, while you organize your family members' birthdays, there are other people having a hard time during the pandemic; that, while you have dinners to gather when such events are currently prohibited, many people are dealing with a disease that takes their loved ones in days, in hours, as has happened to my family with my father's death. How lucky you are not to have to go through something like that. I hope you can maintain that happiness that now accompanies you for a longer time."

"Javier, why are you telling me all this? I called to let you know that I am with you at this moment. Also, my family has indeed gone through something similar because my cousin Mathías was in a coma for several days in the hospital. His recovery was difficult, and we were all very worried at home for him; remember everything I told you about that."

"This is not the same case, Perla. As usual, you make everything revolve around you. The case is quite different. Your cousin is today at home enjoying life, and I am burying my father tomorrow. Now, if you will excuse me, I have many pending things; as you well understand, death does not wait."

At the end of the day, I took Mr. Marlei for a walk. Bella must have noticed that something was wrong because when I returned, she had a lemon verbena tea and some chocolate cakes on the table and was waiting for me to chat.

"Bella, what are you doing awake? I thought you were sleeping."

"No, dear, how do you think I can sleep seeing you so uneasy? I feel you are sad today. What happened, Perla? Is there something I can help you with?"

"No, Bella, nothing happened. Why do you say that?"

"Dear, my dear Perla, you know I've been close to you since the day you were born, and we've lived through many things together. You know well I would have done anything for you not to go through a single sad moment in your life, but there are things that, even if we want with all our might, we can't change. However, there is something I can always do for you, and that is to listen to you."

"I have been trying all day to hide my thoughts, Bella. I do not want to worry you; I do not want you to feel bad because of me. How did you realize that something was happening to me?"

"How do you think I cannot notice when you, my sun, light up the house with your smile every day, but today, instead, the sun did not rise, and there was no smile all day? I could not overlook that. I know something is worrying you, and something has overshadowed you. Tell me, my girl, what is going on?"

I told her what happened with Javier. The guilt was killing me. I didn't want to believe that the one who had been my boyfriend for so many years suddenly became almost a stranger, that on top of that, his dad died, and that to him, I was little less than the culprit because while he suffered, I was partying, according to what he himself had reproached me for.

I felt comforted after talking to Bella. Then I let her go to sleep, but before she left, she gave me a book open to a page that had this phrase underlined from the novel All the Light We Cannot See by Anthony Doerr: "When I lost my sight, Werner, people said I was brave. When my father left, people said I was brave. But it is not bravery; I have no other option. I wake up and live my life. Do you do the same?"

* * *

November 16, 1959

When Raúl realized how much writing this diary helped me, he encouraged me to start this second notebook. He was even the one who gave it to me when he saw I had finished the first one. I believe the promise I made to him to document all our days, not just the good ones, but also the days that upset us, the days that saddened us, the days that pained us, is the reason I have picked up the pen today to continue writing. I have a lump in my throat that makes it hard to breathe.

When my grandparents died, the pain was intense, but at that moment, Raúl had come into my life, illuminating it with his love and tenderness to help me overcome the loss of my *nonni*.

When my mother passed away, I thought I would die along with her; the sadness overwhelmed me, and I did not think I would survive that moment. Even having the responsibility of Alba small by my side, nothing mattered to me. I did not have my mother, and that was killing me. However, Raúl was there to show me with his beautiful love that everything passes, that together we would overcome that misfortune, and that he would be there for me, and so he was. All this time, he has been with me.

Raúl was the one who taught me strength; he was my teacher in the fight, but today my strength is left with him. This morning, my husband died; holding my hand, he took his last breath taken by the whooping cough, although the doctors are still not sure of this diagnosis. His admission to the hospital was very quick, so we thought it would be an asthma attack, but his condition worsened, and they did not let him leave anymore. He was hospitalized for three days, during which they didn't allow me to see him, as they had to confirm what was wrong with him, but knowing that he was in his last moments, I didn't care about anything or anyone. I pushed everyone away like a madwoman, entered his room, and saw him. He was sleeping, but I know he felt me. I screamed his name and held his hand. I wanted him to stand up, to open his little eyes, to look at me, and to tell me, as always, that he was there and that I should not worry because he was with me.

My beloved Raúl, you left when we were still just beginning; we had so much to live for. Now, I do not know what I am going to do without you, without your advice, without your kisses, without your smiles.

Alba has asked about you all day. I cannot speak, and I do not know what to tell her. I just cry, even now without tears, because I have run out, my love. Please, Raúl, help me; tell me what I need to do and how I would live now without you. Why did this have to happen to us? Why to me? I have always done things right; it is not fair. It is not fair that I do not have you now. You left me alone, even knowing that I would not be able to live without you.

VI. After a Storm

June 15, 2020

"Good morning, princess. How are you? I was calling to tell you that we have already confirmed our return tickets to Colombia. We are leaving in fifteen days. We have to take care of several things we left pending, but we hope to return soon."

"Good morning, Dad. I am very well; thanks for asking. Do not worry. I understand. I know you have to return home, though that does not mean I will not miss you a lot. But I am certain it will be as you say and that you will be back soon."

"We will not be able to join you for dinner tonight, but the uncles and Vicente Jr. are going to Bella's house for dinner. Marta is feeling a bit unwell; she has a stomachache. It is nothing serious, but she prefers not to go out today, and I am going to stay with her in case she needs anything."

"That is a shame. I hope she gets better soon so we can see you tomorrow. Please keep me updated on how she is feeling. Also, I wanted to tell you how I am doing with Bella's second diary; it has been a while since we talked about it."

"But tell me, princess, I have free time; tell me everything you want. I have a question: Does Bella know that you are telling me about what you read? I would not like us to be discussing something as personal as her diary without her knowing and approving."

"Of course, she knows, Dad. I told her from day one. In fact, I sense that Bella is interested in me sharing with you what I am reading. I was stunned when I read about Raúl's death. I have not made much progress after that. The pages that follow that event are filled with pain and the need to recover to continue with her life. She emphasizes that she has no other choice but to keep moving forward since she has two young daughters she cannot abandon. I realize how close Aunt Alba was to Bella because, even though she was young, she understood and accompanied her mother at every moment, in every step. It even seemed that decisions about the future were made jointly by Alba and Bella."

After Dad's call, I continued with my day. The afternoon passed between clinic reports and therapies for some of the children I have been seeing these months; the situation for some of them is getting more complicated with the pandemic, and certain cases that were already complex are becoming even more challenging. The isolation of the children does not help with the development of many skills needed to face emotional crises, such as empathy with other human beings, given that they are not having the opportunity to socialize with anyone, only with their close environment, which in many cases is reduced solely to their parents.

I received a message at the end of the afternoon that I cannot deny made me happy to read. It is nice to know that someone is looking forward to seeing us, even if it is through a cell phone screen.

Good afternoon, Perla. I hope you are having a beautiful day. At least today turned out very nicely, with no rain falling and the sun shining brightly. I hope you have not forgotten our virtual cooking date, or rather, you teach me how to cook. I bought all the ingredients you asked for. I hope I did not mix any up. I will call you at seven in the evening, as we agreed. Keep enjoying the day. Take care! See you soon. Salomón.

June 19, 2020

Each day, I am more amazed by Bella's ability to emerge from her gray days; I wonder if I could have had the same strength to face such demanding situations as she did.

Bella's life has seen all shades. After gradually overcoming the loss of her husband Raúl, she now faced her father Antonio's illness. From what I can read in the diary so far, he has been diagnosed with rapidly advancing prostate cancer that is deteriorating his health. The situation is complex for Bella, who has to set aside the suffering she had been enduring due to Raúl's death to accompany her father in his final months.

However, life does not wait, and the girls were growing up. Alba turns eight, while Alondra, at two years old, walks confidently around the house, also uttering her first complete sentences to the delight of her grandfather Antonio, who enjoys the company of his granddaughters. They give him strength with their antics and combined with Bella's affection, they uplift his broken spirit.

Bella, the girls, and Ana, the young woman who helps with raising Alba and Alondra, moved to Antonio's house for a season to accompany him, not only to look after his physical health but also to encourage him in his battle against the disease. From what I can tell, at the beginning of the news, my grandmother had hope that her father would overcome the cancer, as back then, people were not as aware of how dangerous the disease was. However, as I progress in the story, I realize that Bella begins to prepare for Antonio's inevitable departure.

* * *

December 30, 1960

I want to leave a record that I write these lines as fulfillment of the promise I made to my beloved husband. Raúl, being aware at that time that writing helps me to unburden myself, made me promise that I would write my experiences in this notebook, especially in the saddest moments for me. Today is one of those.

The day I was desperately fleeing from has arrived. Several days ago, Dad was admitted to the hospital due to complications from the illness that was attacking him; three days ago, he stopped eating and drinking water. I have been trying by all means to prepare myself for the inevitable, but nothing I did would allow me to be ready for this.

Dad passed away this morning. I have stayed by his bedside all these days. I have had the opportunity to tell him a thousand times how much I love him and how grateful I am to him.

Today, before leaving, he opened his eyes to look at me and smiled. I had his hand held close to my chest. I did not want to let him go, but I understood that he was suffering. The doctors explained to me that in the phase he was in, the illness was very painful, and I did not want or could see him suffer anymore.

I kissed Dad for the last time and said goodbye, whispering in his ear that he could go peacefully and that he should look for Mom and my grandparents and kiss them for me. I am sure they are together now, that reunion was beautiful, and that dad is no longer in pain. He did not deserve to suffer. He has always been an extraordinary man. These last two weeks were hard for him, but he never complained. He did not want me to feel bad. I am convinced that was why he did not say anything. Until the last moment, my dad was concerned about not giving me additional sorrows beyond those we had already experienced at home.

Now, I have to carry on alone with everything that is coming, unlike previous losses where Dad was always by my side to handle the tedious, as well as painful, procedures that family members must deal with after the death of a loved one. Today, however, it is my turn to say goodbye to my father alone, my inseparable companion until the day of his death, my advisor, and my guide.

I feel like I do everything automatically, knowing that now I am the only person who can resolve things and that it is up to me alone to do so.

Dad is no longer here. I have to accept it, although accepting it does not mean it does not burn. It hurts a lot, but tomorrow, the sun will rise again, my girls will keep growing, and they need my help. As long as they need me, I have to be there.

I will wash my face, wipe my tears, and continue my life, always remembering my grandparents, my beloved mother, my beloved Raúl, and now my sweet Antonio.

I am left with the unconditional love of each of you. Your teachings will guide me in every step, and your strength is and will always be an example for me to follow.

Rest in peace, my loves. Now, I have to continue without you physically but with you in my heart until my last days.

* * *

July 4, 2020

I find myself once again moved by the latest readings of my grandmother's diary. The death of her father definitely changed Bella's character, as it was a heavy blow that would take her time to recover, but she rose to continue as she had done before.

I write these lines with my sensitivity on edge. Dad is returning to Colombia, where he has his life, his home, and is happy, but I cannot stop thinking that he will not be here for a while, nor will he leave his scent behind every time we hug, a scent I enjoy so much. I understand that life is like this and that we all have and must follow our path, but as Bella said in her diary, just because I understand it does not mean it does not burn.

He and Marta stopped by my grandmother's house on the way to the airport. The five of us had breakfast together, including Mr. Marlei, who, as always, kissed my father as much as he could. Dad's sadness was noticeable when saying goodbye, but I tried to cheer him up, telling him it was not the first time we were saying goodbye.

"I am going to miss our dinners, Gabo!"

"Do not stop calling me, Perla. I am always thinking of you."

"I love you, Dad, and do not worry about us. You know I will take care of Bella. We will be fine."

"I do not doubt that, dear. I know you are the best thing happening to Bella these days, just as you have always been and continue to be the best thing that has happened to me. I want to ask you, please, not to forget who you are. Don't get distracted on the path for too long, my love. Daisies are beautiful, but if you spend your time plucking them along the way before you know it, several springs will have passed, and you know that the time that goes by doesn't come back. Invest your time wisely so that it bears fruit, not takes life away."

Before dinner, I decided to message Javier, as I wanted to know how he was. I learned from Jane that they had cremated his father. I thought that if I took the first step, Javier would respond. I was wrong: he read my message but did not reply. It is better this way.

On another note, before the day ended, I received a call that brought back my spirits. It was Aunt Alondra who gave me the good news that she would take the room that Dad had left vacant in the rented house when he went to Cartagena; she and Aunt Paloma were going to rent the house for three more months. That made me happy. I am going to have my family close for a little longer. The pleasant thing about all this, moreover, is that with Aunt Alondra and Stefano, her husband, in the house, it is more likely that Mathías, my cousin, will come to visit them. That would be the cherry on top since my cousin and I are close. We get along very well, not just because we are the same age but also because we have many things in common, which makes our conversations very entertaining. I eagerly look forward to seeing them around here these days.

$$* \ * \ *$$

February 7, 1961

It has been a little over a month since my father's death, and slowly, life is returning to its course for me. I understand that in the end, it is like this: we, the ones left behind, suffer, as those who leave are in a better place.

Today, I met a man who caught my attention while I was buying some things for Alba's eighth birthday, which will be in a couple of weeks; I want to do something small but meaningful for her. I am still in mourning, but I think this would be an opportune occasion to distract ourselves at home and forget a bit about the past few months, which have been so difficult for everyone, including my precious Alba.

Returning to the topic of the man, he introduced himself, and we talked a bit. His name is Rafael. From the details of his physical appearance, he seems to be of Japanese descent. Something that caught our attention was finding out that we are both twenty-nine years old and also share the same birthday: we were both born on June 5, 1931. He said to me, "This year, we will celebrate together," and I laughed to show him that I had no intention of celebrating my birthday, especially not with a stranger. But he looked straight into my eyes as if tempting fate to ensure that what he said would come true.

Rafael insisted on accompanying me to finish buying everything I needed and even insisted on bringing me to my doorstep. He drives a lovely cream-colored Cadillac. When I asked him what he did for a living, he replied that he had a family business dedicated to importing cars.

As we said goodbye, he asked me who I lived with; I told him with my two daughters. He got scared, thinking I was married, but I did not give him any more information about that. I prefer that he assumes I am married, so I do not have to see him again. At this moment in my life, I have no desire to think about anything new.

* * *

December 2, 1961

All of Rafael's efforts have borne fruit. Since I met him at the beginning of this year, he has not stopped courting me; he has taken on the task of winning me over and has succeeded despite my resistance, as I still did not feel ready to love anyone else after Raúl. Moreover, I thought it would be difficult for my girls to see another man around, but that has not been the case.

Rafael has managed to win the affection of my little ones, and that puts me at ease. Seeing my daughters enjoy his company is a beautiful gift he gives me without knowing it.

Yesterday afternoon, I accepted his proposal to be his girlfriend. We went out to dinner to celebrate, even bringing Ana along, who remains faithfully by my side, helping me at home with the girls and other chores. The night was perfect. I saw my daughters happy, especially Alba, who is already a big girl and understands everything. When I was able to talk to her today, before she went to school, she told me she was happy to know we have someone to protect us and that she liked knowing I could now be safer. It broke my heart to know that my daughter was worried about me in that way; it hurt to realize that, without intending to, I had made her part of everything I have been through over the years. I should not have; she is just a little girl who should not have to know about adult problems, but it was impossible to hide anything from her since Alba is so mature that she understands everything even without a single word being said.

At least now, I am moving forward without fear, as I hope that Rafael will be the man who gives us the security we are looking for—not just me, but Alba as well. My mother always said, "There's something that never fails after a storm; no matter how dark and strong it is, the sun always comes out the next day."

* * *

July 5, 2020

The only blonde in the family, with black eyes terribly similar to my grandmother's but slightly slanted, is Paloma, Bella's daughter with Rafael. By profession, a homemaker, Paloma has inherited Bella's sparkle; she seems like a shooting star, leaving light wherever she walks. She turned fifty-seven this year and is married to Vicente, who is of Argentine descent; his family is from Mendoza, in the west of the country.

Paloma and Vicente have two children: Antonio, the eldest at twenty-five, and Vicente Jr., seventeen, who was named after his father after several discussions, as Aunt Paloma disagreed with naming children after their parents. She believes that doing so imposes a burden on them that they do not deserve, a burden attached to the name. Vicente, on the other hand, wanted to name him after himself to honor the family tradition of naming one of the sons after the ancestors.

From an early age, Paloma was very cheerful and lively; she loved to act, dance, and sing at home, always becoming the center of attention at any gathering or celebration she attended. It was one afternoon at a close friend's house that she met Vicente, who fell in love with her spark, her brilliance, and her joy, which seemed endless.

Paloma studied pedagogy but never worked in the field. She dedicated herself to her husband and children, always happy with her role. She accompanied her children throughout their development, making them wonderful kids with talents and skills. At home, we always say that Aunt Paloma's children can do everything and do it very well.

When Vicente Jr. was almost five years old, Paloma discovered her husband's infidelity with another woman. By the time the story of Vicente and his lover became known, they had been having a clandestine affair for almost a year.

I cannot imagine Aunt Paloma's pain upon discovering what had happened, as after dedicating herself entirely to her home and husband, finding out that he was paying her back with betrayal seemed unjust. Nevertheless, it happened, and from what my aunt and I discussed on several occasions, it was a pain she could not bear. She asked her husband for a divorce almost immediately, without asking for any explanation.

We found out shortly after what had happened in detail regarding Vicente's misstep. It turned out that, at that time, he was working as a professor at a university where he met the woman who would become his lover and for whom he would lose his family.

The woman he was seeing in secret turned out to be ten years younger than him, and according to reports, she fell in love with Vicente from the first day she saw him, turning the admiration she felt for her professor into what she believed was love, eventually leading to obsession.

We also learned that Vicente had tried to break up with the young woman several times, but her threats to tell his family what had happened prevented him from ending the relationship.

In the end, which is exactly what happened: the lover, in a fit of jealousy, decided to call Aunt Paloma and tell her everything in detail. My aunt could not finish listening to what she was telling her; she dropped the phone on the floor and ran to Bella to seek help.

Paloma's divorce was painful for everyone, especially for the couple of spouses who suffered greatly from the separation. Vicente, for his part, never abandoned his responsibilities toward his children and his ex-wife. He always looked out for their well-being, not only financially but also emotionally. This is why Vicente appears in family photos from those years and at all important family moments. Despite being legally divorced, he was there, ensuring they were well taken care of.

After the divorce, neither of them was seen with another partner. After almost ten years since their separation, Paloma and Vicente overcame that episode in their relationship and reunite. They married again in a very emotional wedding where we all went through a carousel of emotions with them. It was a ceremony filled with pure love, the same love that still exists in their relationship today, the kind that is felt when being near them because they still share that knowing smile when they talk, because they still hold hands when they walk, because they never miss giving each other a goodnight kiss before sleeping, and because both are, equally, the driving force of their family.

I uniquely adore Aunt Paloma. Although for many, she leads a simple life as a homemaker with her children and husband, to me, she is more than that. She transforms that routine, painting it with a rainbow every day. Through her, I learned to appreciate the vastness of the every day, the greatness of the simple, and the details of daily life.

Aunt Paloma, with a smile, always repeats to me what she once read in *The Book of Joy*: "If you think you are too small to make a difference, try sleeping with a mosquito."

VII. For Love

March 8, 1962

Rafael and I got married today at ten in the morning in the city of Lima amidst a rather tense atmosphere that the country is currently experiencing, soon to hold presidential elections. For this reason, and because Rafael's company has some business with the Peruvian government, we have decided to be discreet with the marriage, which for me has been very convenient, as I do not much like the idea of extravagance. Moreover, I prefer that our lives be more private, as it will be better for the family.

My daughters have been happy to celebrate our union, and this is a source of joy for my heart. On the other hand, Rafael's parents were unable to attend the marriage, with the excuse that they are elderly people who cannot leave home for a long time. However, months before our wedding, I met a couple of close friends of Rafael and his family. Andrea, the wife, told me that it seemed his parents were not happy with our engagement, as they would have preferred a single woman for their son and not a widow with children.

I suppose it has been difficult for my husband to deal with this issue in his family; nevertheless, our affection has been more powerful, and we managed to reach the altar.

Tomorrow, we will leave for our honeymoon. We have decided to go for a few days to the north of Peru to enjoy the beaches and the food of that area. Rafael had proposed leaving the country for a week, going to Argentina or Chile. I have been able to read in his eyes the concern about the current political situation and how it affects his business. Because of this uncertainty, I preferred something nearby; there would be plenty of time to travel later. Moreover, the girls will stay alone with Ana at home, and that also worries me. I don't want to be away from them for so long.

January 4, 1963

It is a special day; my third daughter has been born, and she will be named Paloma. Rafael chose the name, knowing my love for birds. Paloma was born a bit smaller than she should have been, and she also has trouble latching onto the breast, but we are working on that so it does not affect her development. The doctor has asked me to inform him of any details I might notice in these first days. I hope everything continues to evolve correctly.

Rafael is excited about our baby. He does not stop holding her, kissing her, and caressing her. When he hears her cry, he runs to lift her in his arms and then places her on my chest. It moves me to see the concern he has for the baby. He says he has never seen such a beautiful baby before. Not just because she is my child, but I also believe it is true. Paloma was born beautiful, with almond-shaped eyes, light hair, and a round face, so small and fragile, but when she cries, she does so with great strength, as if her life depended on it.

I thank heaven for the joy of a third daughter in the family. I can't help but think how happy my mother would have been with my three princesses; she would have loved them so much. The same is true with my father. I know he would be delighted with the birth of this third little one and happy to see his first two granddaughters becoming the noble girls they are now. He would also be proud of how I have been able to move forward despite everything, and I am sure he would like Rafael, both having conversations about politics, which he was so passionate about.

Sometimes, I think of Raúl and feel a bit guilty as if somehow I am betraying his memory with another man, now even married and with a new baby. Some days, before I sleep, I find myself talking to him, explaining that he will always have a place in my heart but that his daughters and I needed someone by our side, support, help, security, and company, and that, although I denied it at first, in time I understood it was the best for us. Sometimes, I even feel that he responds to me, telling me to be calm and that he trusts my decision is the best. I feel his love, and with that, I fall asleep, as if deep down I know he forgives me.

January 11, 1963

It has been a week since Paloma was born. I had an appointment with her pediatrician because, since she was born small, the doctor needed to follow up to see if everything was going well with her development.

Rafael could not accompany me because he had to leave urgently on a business trip. I went alone to the appointment with Paloma in my arms; one of Rafael's company's employees, who usually assists us when Rafael is away, took us there so he could drive us around the city or help us with any situation that might arise.

Something happened at the appointment for which I was not prepared.

"Isabella, right? A rather graceful woman asked me, sitting next to me. She was very well dressed and looked a little younger than me."

"Yes, is the doctor calling me?" I asked, confusing the woman who spoke to me with the pediatrician's assistant.

"No, no, I don't work here. I would like to have a few words with you if you don't mind."

"Now? What is it about? I'm waiting for the pediatrician to call us."

"Yes, I understand. Don't worry, I'll wait for you here until you're done with the appointment. Maybe we can talk at the café on the corner. Let me introduce myself: my name is María del Carmen García García, and I would like to talk to you about Rafael Tanaka."

During Paloma's pediatric appointment, I couldn't stay calm. I couldn't pay attention to what the doctor was telling me, and he even noticed and asked if I was feeling well. The truth is that I wasn't feeling well; everything was spinning, and I started to sweat cold. I wondered who that woman could be and what she wanted to tell me about my husband. I imagined that something had happened to him, thinking that I couldn't be that unlucky. It wasn't fair that I had to go through the pain of losing my husband again.

I left the office, almost running with my baby in my arms, hoping to find that woman to finally know what she had to tell me.

"Isabella, I'm here."

"Tell me, where are we going to talk?"

"Here, follow me. I've already reserved a table for us to sit at. Look, Isabella, I know you don't know me; you have no idea who I am. I've introduced myself, but that means nothing to you, I understand. On the other hand, I do know who you are; I've known since a year ago when you married Rafael. I don't want to turn this story into a tragedy. On the contrary, I want to go straight to the point we have in common so as not to waste your time. I know you have two small daughters at home who are waiting for you."

"Please tell me at once what you want to say. All this is making me nervous. Besides, it's almost time to feed my baby; I don't want her to start crying."

"Isabella, I am two months pregnant. The father of my baby is Rafael. He and I had a relationship for almost five years when he met you. We were engaged, and we were going to get married in mid-1961, but you appeared in our lives that year and changed everything."

"What are you telling me? I am married to Rafael. We got married a year ago, and I just gave birth to our daughter. We love each other."

"I know all that, Isabella. Believe me, I know, but what I'm telling you is true: I am pregnant with Rafael. Since you met, we have not stopped seeing each other. We meet every so often when he travels to deal with his company's matters. I live in Chiclayo with my family. My parents and his parents are close friends. His parents never accepted your marriage to him; you know that. Moreover, he has come to look for me now that he is in the north, but he hasn't found me. He doesn't know that I am here in Lima. Please, Isabella, listen to me. I have to tell you something, and I have to ask you something." María del Carmen pleaded with tears in her eyes, holding my hand.

"No, I can't listen to you anymore. I need Rafael to explain what you're talking about, and you can't come looking for me like this to tell me all this."

"Isabella, please don't go, and just listen to this last thing I want to say. I need you to think about what I'm going to ask you. I beg you, please let Rafael go. He is confused, but it's me he loves.

We are going to have a child. You already have your daughters, your house, and your things, and you had your life before you met Rafael, but I have no one. My life is Rafael. I have known him since we were six years old, and since that day, my dream has been to marry him and to form the family we both wanted so much, but you appeared in our lives and took everything away. You took everything that is mine and what belongs to me. Please understand that I have his child in my womb now. If you don't let him go, I will die, and my child will die with me; you will be responsible for that, and you will carry it with you forever. Let Rafael go; I beg you, Isabella. Let him be with me. He doesn't live in peace, and he has no tranquility living with you. Let him be happy by my side."

I didn't listen to her anymore. I stood up to go in search of our vehicle that would bring me back home. On the way back, I couldn't hold back the tears. I cried so much that the driver asked if everything was alright with the baby. I couldn't answer him; I just felt the tears streaming down my face.

* * *

July 24, 2020

"Good morning, Bella. How did you wake up? I ordered cheese bread from the bakery we love, and by the way, the coffee I brewed is special. My dad brought it from Cartagena when he came, but I hadn't opened it until we finished what we already had in the pantry."

"It smells delicious, Perla. Let me sit with you to savor all this. You went to bed late last night, didn't you? I got up a couple of times to go to the bathroom and saw your reading light on in your room. Did you have some work pending?"

"A bit of everything, though truthfully, I stayed up mainly reading your diary and your stories, Bella. Even though I've always known some of them, reading in detail from your perspective what was happening, as well as what you felt at the moment, is different; it leaves me speechless. What strength, Grandma! Where can one draw all that resilience to face demanding situations?"

"Perla, dear, I always tell you, if you have the chance to travel, do it!"

"Yes, Grandma, of course, the times I've traveled, I've done so with that advice of yours in mind, but what does that have to do with what I just said?"

"I'm going to tell you an anecdote from a trip I took to the Canary Islands about thirty years ago when I had the chance to visit Tenerife. You know I've always liked to travel to learn about diverse cultures; I feel that the best way to learn about tolerance is by experiencing diverse cultures or beliefs. I believe we cannot talk about love or respect for something we do not know that we have not perceived with our own eyes. That's why I traveled because traveling made my love for humanity and nature grow. On that trip to Tenerife, I was told a story that I instantly identified with. A local guide from the island took me to see a lush forest of Canarian pines. What my eyes could see was a masterpiece in all its splendor. The place was surrounded by huge pines that also gave off a unique aroma; they smelled of life. When the guide told me about the peculiarity of this pine, I was stunned. These trees had a special characteristic that allowed them to stay alive, even though they lived in a volcanic area that constantly suffered from wildfires that devastated much of the vegetation in the area.

Their peculiarity is that the Canarian pine is fire-resistant. This pine has three important characteristics that make it resistant. The first is its thicker-than-normal bark, which it uses to protect its core in extreme cases. The second is the pine nuts, which are the seeds of the pine; these are housed in the pinecones, which have a winged appendix that can be detached and launched long distances by the force of the wind, and in case an intense fire destroys the tree, the pine nuts that flew off sprout in another area that hasn't been affected by the fire and are reborn in another field. Lastly, its living cells, which may be the key to everything. This tree is capable of maintaining living cells inside the wood, so even if the fire has burned all its leaves, it can regrow from within and bear fruit again.

That's the same thing I've done all these years, Perla; I've kept my living cells inside my soul. I've protected them because I knew the fire wouldn't last forever, and so when the fire passed, I used them to regrow, and here I am, blossomed."

I finished the day, and the image of Solomon came to mind. I remembered that we had agreed to communicate these days, so I sent him a text message:

"Hi, Solomon. How are you? I hope I'm not bothering you. I just wanted to know how you were. Maybe you have some free time one of these days to resume the cooking classes; I was thinking that if you agree, we could even have the class in person. Have a nice night. Take care."

August 4, 2020

"Hi, Perla, good morning. How are you? I read your message yesterday, but it was a bit late to respond, and I didn't want to wake you, so I preferred to call you early today."

"Hey, Solomon. I'm very well; thank you for asking. How are you?"

"I'm good too, just a bit worried."

"Worried about what? What happened?"

"It's just that I don't like having unfinished business, especially when it comes to cooking classes," Solomon replied with a hint of mischief.

"I understand. I said, laughing. I'm the same way. I don't like having anything pending; it makes me tense."

"So, Perla, you decide."

"Let me call you at the end of the day, okay? Today I have to take Bella to my aunt's house, where she'll stay for a few days. We'll see how long Bella can tolerate another bed that's not hers. I won't be able to stay with them; I have a couple of important meetings these days that require space and tranquility, and at my aunts' house, it's difficult, with all the commotion they bring, chatting and laughing nonstop."

"Perfect. So, what do you think if I visit you tomorrow, considering you won't have company for dinner? I wouldn't want you to feel lonely. Send me the list of things we need for the cooking classes, and I'll take care of everything. See you tomorrow."

August 7, 2020

I started the day early as usual and tried to do my morning meditation, but I felt weak and had a sore throat, which I tried to ignore. After a while, I walked to the kitchen to prepare breakfast, but I realized that I couldn't smell the coffee brewing in my grandmother's French press. That caught my attention because the coffee we were using was the one Dad brought from Colombia, known for its intense aroma. I got quite worried, to the point that I felt sudden dizziness and had to hold onto the wall to avoid falling. I quickly grabbed my phone to call my cousin Mathías, who had experienced something similar when he had COVID-19. Without realizing it, my whole body was shaking so much that I couldn't unlock my phone because my fingers weren't hitting the right numbers.

"Mathi, I'm glad you answered quickly; it's Perla."

"Hey, cousin, of course, I have your number saved. Are you okay? You sound nervous."

"Mathi, I've lost my sense of smell. It started this morning. I can't smell anything; plus, my throat hurts, and I have a bad headache. I'm calling because I'm worried and want to know how you realized you had COVID-19."

"Perla, the first thing you need to do is calm down. Let me find a place near Bella's house where you can get a rapid test to clear up any doubts. Once we have the result, we'll see what to do, but you need to stay calm. You're young and healthy, so if you've caught something, you'll get through it quickly. Don't worry."

Mathías sent me the address where I needed to go for the test. When I arrived at the park, there was an extensive line, which was done without getting out of the car. After almost two hours, it was my turn; the attendants wrote a number on the car's windshield, indicating where to go for the test. After reaching the designated spot, two people fully covered in special suits from head to toe approached, with only their faces covered by some sort of transparent plastic to allow them to see. The first person took the data of the person being tested and handed over a code to be scanned with a cell phone, directing to a website where the number given during the test should be recorded to later see the respective result.

The second person approached with a kind of swab to insert into the nasal cavities, collecting the sample for the COVID-19 test.

It took about three hours to get the result. They seemed like the longest three hours of my life. The wait was endless. I couldn't concentrate on anything; I was quite scared. When I received the result, I called my cousin to confirm that it was positive for coronavirus.

Mathi guided me through the process of calming down, sent me the instructions I should follow, and advised me that if at any moment I started to feel shortness of breath, high fevers, or any new symptoms different from the ones I already had, I should immediately contact him to coordinate a visit to the hospital for an emergency. I did everything my cousin suggested, starting by calling my primary doctor in Colorado to inform him about the positive coronavirus test result.

Next, I called my dad to tell him what was happening while Mathi called Aunt Alondra, as we thought it was necessary for everyone in the rented house to also get tested to rule out any contagion, especially Bella, who was the most vulnerable.

Now it's almost eleven at night, and we have confirmed that everyone in the rented house is negative, so I'm much calmer. As for me, I haven't had any additional symptoms apart from the loss of smell and sore throat, although the latter has worsened a bit. I'm already taking the medicine the doctor sent home shortly after finishing the phone call with him.

I also talked to Solomon so he could get tested. He will do it early tomorrow at the hospital, although he assured me that he feels quite well. He said he would be available for anything I need and that I should keep him informed; he also told me to take advantage of the time to rest, which I haven't been able to do until now.

Getting sick always makes me very tense, especially knowing that this illness has taken many people I know. It scares me to know that one of the characteristics of the coronavirus is the speed and ferocity with which it progresses in the body, worsening its victim very quickly, to the point of being slightly sick one day and hospitalized, intubated, and in a coma the next.

- The coronavirus pandemic continues to dominate the news.

- The health department has reported 1,683 infections and one death in the last 24 hours.

- There are six COVID-19 vaccine candidates in "very advanced" stages, so there is hope that the population will soon be immunized against the coronavirus.

- In Spain, more than 50,000 healthcare workers have been infected, 20,000 deaths have occurred in nursing homes, and there is excess mortality of 44,000 people in a population of forty-seven million with one of the best health systems in the world.

- The United States government announced on Thursday that it is lifting its recommendation to avoid travel to all countries due to the coronavirus, replacing it with individual recommendations like the one issued for Spain, advising its citizens to "reconsider" traveling to the country.

- After several months of declining numbers, COVID-19 cases, hospitalizations, and deaths are on the rise again in the United States.

* * *

March 20, 1963

Rafael came to pick me up to take Paloma and me to the scheduled appointment with the pediatrician. My baby is growing fast, and that makes us happy. At the appointment, the doctor told us that Paloma was developing normally and had even reached her corresponding average percentile, so we left the office feeling reassured. However, Rafael and I had many things to discuss. Since I asked him to leave the house that night, he returned from his trip. The same day, I found out about his relationship with another woman; we hadn't talked about it. Our conversations were basically limited to discussing Paloma.

"Bella, do you have a few minutes, please? I would like to talk to you alone. If you want, we can go out for a while. It won't take long, I promise."

"Rafael, I don't want to leave the house and leave Paloma alone. She will need her milk soon, and if I'm not nearby, she will cry a lot. I don't like knowing that she's crying from hunger."

"Don't worry, we can talk here in the house then. Let's go to the living room for a moment, okay?"

"Let me start, Rafael. I have a lot of things I want to say. First, these past two months have been terrible for me. I can't remember nights as difficult as the ones I've had since all this happened. And I've had difficult nights before, but none like these. You, more than anyone, know everything I've been through in recent years—the deep pain I felt with the loss of my husband, which left me with two small girls, so I've had to play the role of both mother and father for them."

"As if that weren't enough, you met me when I was still mourning my father's death, a death that left an unprecedented emptiness in my soul. It was you who helped me heal, but none of that mattered to you because, knowing all the details about my past, you played with me, with my love, with my heart, and worse, with my daughters' hearts. You trampled on us and separated us forever."

"Bella, I know none of this is easy for you to understand, but please don't think that I'm not suffering. I'm terribly hurt by all of this. I miss you a lot. I miss the girls and our life together. I've made a terrible mistake by not knowing how to make decisions, but believe it or not, the last thing I wanted was to hurt you. In the end, I hurt everyone, especially you, the woman I've loved the most in my life, the one I still love and will love until the end of my days. Come with me, Bella; come with the girls. Let's leave the country.

Give me that chance. I have a proposal for us to move to Chile; we can leave in two weeks. Let's prepare everything. The business is expanding, and my partners want me to go to Chile for a while. Let's all go, please. Think about it. Tell me you'll think about it, that we'll give ourselves the chance to start over far away from everything." Rafael took my hand tightly, tears in his eyes, begging me to consider it.

"Paloma has woken up. I need to see her; she must be hungry. But rest assured, I will think about it. Come back in a couple of days, and you'll have an answer."

March 28, 1963

We arrived in Chile this morning. The trip was quite smooth, more than I expected. It took a little over four hours, if I'm not mistaken, to get from Lima to Santiago by plane. The girls endured the flight without any issues, thanks to Rafael, who helped a lot throughout the process from the beginning of this journey. Additionally, we brought Ana with us, who supported us by running alongside us to achieve the move from Lima to Santiago de Chile in record time.

Today, while strolling a bit through the city of Santiago, I was pleasantly surprised by the cleanliness of its streets and the friendliness of its people. We have arrived in the last month of summer, so the weather is quite good. I was told that the temperature might drop a bit at night, but overall, it's very pleasant to go for a walk in the city. I find this city very pleasing, with orderly streets where the mountain range stands out and can be seen throughout the city's journey, making the walk a visual spectacle. At lunchtime, some Chilean friends of Rafael invited us to the Union Club, where we had a delicious meal and enjoyed a beautiful afternoon with my little ones, who were happy, especially Alba. Since she is the eldest, she realizes everything and understands that this trip will reunite us with Rafael, which makes her quite excited.

The city generally has a festive atmosphere as it prepares for the upcoming municipal elections. That is the main topic on the front pages of the newspapers and the subject of conversations when people gather to socialize.

I still have a lot of work to do at home, like unpacking clothes and organizing the home where we will be staying for now. For now, we have the basics to be comfortable for the first few weeks, but later on, we will have to buy some things for the house when we know what exactly we need.

VIII. A New Story

August 22, 2020

It has been fifteen days since my COVID-19 test came back positive. Today, I was finally able to leave the house, and the first thing I did was go to the park to take a new test. After that, I stopped by the gas station to fill up my car's tank because, after so many days in quarantine, I hadn't realized it was empty. While there, I received a text message with the result of the coronavirus test I had just taken at the park: "Negative."

The first thing I did was forward the result to my family chat group, and everyone celebrated the news with me. I could finally be at peace knowing my body was free of the virus. I felt happy and grateful for having overcome the illness, knowing many people hadn't; for the family I have, who supported and cared for me throughout the quarantine; and for Mr. Marlei, who has been my closest and most important emotional support during these fifteen days, though in truth, he has been since the first day I offered to take care of him.

As I was feeling grateful, Salomón came to mind. From the first day, I tested positive for COVID-19, he never stopped calling to check on what I needed, and he even sent food to my home on several occasions. I even received flowers and a card wishing me a speedy recovery.

I talked to Jane in the late afternoon; we discussed many personal things, as well as the usual topics about the clinic. I thanked her for her concern and support during the days I felt ill. I told her how important her friendship and affection were to me. Today, I know I mustn't take anything for granted; COVID-19 has made that clear to me: we are here today, but tomorrow is not guaranteed.

This reminded me of what my teacher used to repeat during meditation sessions, which took me so long to internalize: "Absolutely everything we feel will pass, both the soul-piercing sadness and the happiness that seems to stay. A moment of happiness is followed by one of sorrow, and a moment of crisis is followed by one of rebuilding, for those who dare not to remain eternally identified with a single emotion or situation."

A moment ago, the company I hired to disinfect the house called; they will come with special machines to go through all the rooms. Before Bella returns to me, I want to be very sure there is no trace of the virus left. The appointment is for early tomorrow morning when I will be walking Mr. Marlei. They told me the products they use are not toxic to humans or pets, but I prefer to be out of the house when they come, especially for Mr. Marlei.

I will call Aunt Paloma to coordinate the details of my grandmother's return to her home.

"Perla, dear, we are happy that everything turned out well; we expected nothing less, but it still makes us happy to confirm it."

"Thank you so much, Aunt. You are one more reason everything turned out well in this process."

"Trust, dear, that the plans life has for you are great; there is no need to despair. I know it sounds cliché, but everything comes at its due time."

"It's hard for me not to despair... You know how my character is, though it's ironic because, as a psychologist, I help people in their crises; yet, sometimes, I struggle to help myself. But don't worry, Aunt, I'm trying."

"Tell me, Perla, how are you now? I don't mean your physical health. Tell me how things are with Javier. What has happened to him in these days?"

"Oh, Aunt, you know I get more confused every day. I told you I had doubts about my relationship with him, but when he asked for time, it affected me; even though I later found out he was seeing another girl, it hurt a lot. I assumed it was my wounded ego, but the doubts didn't go away; instead, they settled more strongly in my mind. In recent days, Salomón has appeared in my life, who, without intending to, has been gaining space; now I smile when I receive a message from him, and that worries me too because, if I don't get back with Javier, I don't think I'm ready to start a new relationship yet. It's a very confusing situation; I know I'm the only one who can resolve this, but I haven't given myself the time to think clearly out of fear of the answer."

"You are absolutely right, Perla; only you can know what is in your heart, but for that, you must be calm because you can only hear the heart's beats when there is no noise. Clear your mind and listen to yourself; the only way tomorrow can play against you and hurt you is if you let worry settle in."

"Thanks for listening, Aunt. For now, I only have one thing clear, and that is I don't want to return to Colorado yet; something tells me that here I am in the process of discovering what I still need to do, and we will be close for a little longer. It will be a joy for me to continue enjoying your company."

September 1, 2020

"Good morning, Gabo. I woke up thinking about you today. I dreamed about you all night that we were sailing around the islands of Cartagena over those beautiful blue seas, enjoying the music as we always do, and talking about everything. It made me very happy to see myself so content by your side, as I always am when we're together."

"*Buongiorno, principessa! Stanotte ti ho sognata tutta la notte, eravamo al cinema e avevi quel maglione rosa che mi piace tanto! Non penso che a te, principessa, penso sempre a te.*" Gabriel replied with a mix of joy and nostalgia.

"I love that movie, Dad. It's so nice that you reminded me of it. How do you manage to always be so special to me?"

"Do you doubt that you deserve all my love and more? Never doubt it, Perla; be certain that it is so."

"Thank you, Gabo; always thank you! Besides saying hello, I called because we had an unfinished conversation. Do you have time now?"

"Of course, dear, I always have time to talk with you. We were supposed to discuss your progress in Mom's journal. We left off at how terrible it was for Bella to find out that Rafael was cheating on her and that he had a baby on the way with that other woman, just when your grandmother had just had Paloma."

"Yes, Gabo, that's so awful. I still can't understand why Rafael, loving Bella as he seemed to, did something like that. I'm not judging him. I know people understand the meaning of love differently, although love is the same in reality. Anyway, after that, she wrote that she managed to forgive Rafael and that they even left Peru for Chile to start a kind of new life. From what I read, the family quickly settled into the routine in Santiago within the first few weeks. I was glad, although it did surprise me. I had no idea that Bella had lived with my aunts in Chile. She never mentioned anything about it to me."

"Yes, it's true, dear. Your grandmother did spend some time in Chile, but from what I understand, it was a short season. She returned to Peru quite quickly; in fact, if I remember correctly, she came back after another separation from Rafael, and this one was final."

September 17, 2020

Salomón invited me to spend the weekend in Key West, an island city that, along with several others, forms the Florida Keys archipelago. It is the southernmost point of the state, about 233 kilometers from Cuba. It is quite picturesque, with its wooden houses mostly painted in pastel colors, giving it a friendly and peaceful look. Key West is exceedingly popular with tourists as it is an important stop on several cruise routes in the country. It is known for its coral reefs, admired by many diving professionals and enthusiasts, among other water sports. Key West can be accessed not only by sea but also by road from the city of Weston, where I currently live. When driving, the trip takes about three and a half hours without any stops.

Salomón told me he had planned a trip with his sister and nephew, whom he loves so much. He always tells me stories about the little one whenever he can. However, his sister couldn't visit him due to the pandemic, and the trip with them was canceled. For that trip, Salomón had rented an RV, with which they would drive to one of the beaches in Key West specially equipped for these vehicles, where they would spend three days and two nights.

Now, Salomón suggested that I accompany him since everything was already reserved and paid for. He didn't want to miss the trip.

I can't deny that the idea of the trip is appealing to me. I had never driven an RV before; worse still, I don't even remember ever getting into one before, so I quickly thought of saying yes, but something held me back. I think I haven't given myself time to reflect on what happened the last time we saw each other at my house when we agreed to cook dinner together.

That day, everything was going normally. Salomón arrived at the agreed time, bringing the ingredients to prepare dinner at Bella's house. We were alone, as we knew we would be, although I must admit that I hadn't thought at the time that things would take that turn.

I don't mean to say that Salomón isn't attractive; on the contrary, I find him very handsome, but up until that moment, our relationship had been characterized by respecting our friendship without any hints of anything else, so I didn't expect that day to be different.

I had decided to cook something simple, without strong smells, because my grandmother's apartment is small, and I didn't want the smell of food to permeate everywhere. The cooking time was very pleasant; we talked about many topics, including family matters for both of us, sharing a bit about where we come from, where we grew up, and what we studied, as well as a brief introduction to our parents, his siblings in his case, and my aunts in mine.

I confess that I really liked what Salomón shared about his family because I could see that he was a man who loved and respected his home, and I identified with that. Up until that moment, everything was going as I had thought.

At the end of dinner, without realizing it, the playlist that I had set as background music started playing songs in Spanish, a language Salomón wasn't very proficient in, not to say that his knowledge of it was limited to four or five basic sentences. The music player played Julio Iglesias's song, "Me Olvidé de Vivir:"

> *De tanto correr por la vida sin freno*
> *me olvidé que la vida se vive un momento.*
> *De tanto querer ser en todo el primero*
> *me olvidé de vivir los detalles pequeños.*

When I finished translating the song for Salomón, I turned my face to comment on the lyrics with him, and then I realized that his eyes had welled up with tears that hadn't fallen yet. My immediate reaction was to seek his arms and move closer to him to somehow console him in an attempt to tell him that I understood his sensitivity to that song because it also gave me goosebumps. As the years go by, the song becomes more real to me.

De tanto correr por ganar tiempo al tiempo,
me olvidé de vivir.

Without realizing it, one thing led to another, and we ended up kissing in what was the most tender kiss I had experienced up until that moment. I felt Salomón's warm lips as they began to brush against mine. I didn't even try to put an end to the situation. On the contrary, I think I was the one who, noticing some hesitation in Salomón's advance, moved closer to him with the intention that the kiss would be inevitable for both of us. If it weren't for my phone ringing, I think I would have decided to take the next step, but the ring somehow made us react and separate.

After what happened, we tried, unsuccessfully, to make the conversation as natural and friendly as it had been before the kiss; however, we both felt that it would no longer be that way.

"So, Perla, what do you say about coming with me to the Keys? We would have to leave tomorrow morning and return on Sunday at the end of the day. I even thought we could bring Mr. Marlei. I know you don't like leaving Bella the task of walking and feeding him."

"I really like the idea, Salomon; even thinking about Mr. Marlei is very thoughtful of you, but..."

"Perla, the RV has two bedrooms. You can have the room that's most comfortable for you. Both have private bathrooms, but I don't want you to feel pressured. On the contrary, I thought of you because you mentioned that you don't know much about Florida, and this would be a nice opportunity for you to see other cities."

"You're right, no longer need to say. I'll be ready tomorrow. I'll make arrangements for one of my aunts to stay at home with Bella. Thanks for thinking of us to accompany you on the trip, Salomón."

* * *

June 5, 1963

"Hello, Isabella, it's María del Carmen speaking. I know you remember me. Please don't hang up; we need to talk."

"How did you get this number? You have no reason to call our house. I live here with my daughters, and the last thing I want is for them to suffer or feel any pain because of you. Leave us alone, please. Rafael has told me your entire story, and I know he doesn't love you. Let him live in peace. We are happy. Don't call again."

"Please, Isabella, listen to me, and don't hang up, I beg you. As you said, what we both want is Rafael's happiness, but also that of our children. You know I'm expecting a baby; it will be a boy, and I will name him Rafael. He will be born in the coming days. Just let me tell you the reason for my call, please, and then I will hang up, and everything will be in your hands." María del Carmen replied with a trembling voice, sobbing.

"Tell me quickly what you want to say; I have many things to do."

"I am calling to ask you to reconsider, please. I don't know exactly what Rafael has told you, but you know he is an older and intelligent man. It is not possible for you to believe that I, who am seven years younger than him, could have tricked him into anything. On the contrary, I started dating Rafael when I was fourteen and he was twenty-one. That was almost ten years ago. Since the first day we met, I couldn't separate from him. We have maintained a relationship throughout all these years, and he has been the only man in my life. As a result of that relationship, I am now pregnant.

You have no idea how I feel; I am now a symbol of shame in my family for being pregnant without being married, and even worse, knowing that Rafael has fled from his responsibility to me and our child. He has abandoned us, and you have allowed all this. You are being complicit in his cowardice."

"I am not complicit with anyone. You knew well that he didn't love you, and yet you insisted on continuing to the point of wanting to have a child. When we met, I didn't know he was seeing you; otherwise, I would never have started anything with him. But now things are different. Today, I know that Rafael ended his relationship with you before starting something with me—that he even asked you not to look for him anymore, but you insisted. And, even worse, I know that when you found out we were getting married, you became his shadow, pursuing him wherever you could until you managed to get pregnant."

"How can you reproach me for that, Isabella? It takes two people to have a baby. I never forced Rafael into anything. I indeed got desperate when I found out he was marrying you because I realized I would lose him forever, and the sorrow clouded my judgment. However, when I sought him out, he didn't refuse to see me. That's how we continued being together all this time, even before his trip to Chile. But at that moment, he didn't tell me anything about his plans to leave the baby and me. His parents were surprised to know that Rafael was no longer in Lima and that he had moved to Chile with you."

"I have nothing more to listen to. Don't call our house again. If you are as close to Rafael's parents as you say, ask them to help you with your child. I can't do anything; I'm deeply sorry. You should have thought things through before accepting scraps from a man who doesn't love you."

"Isabella, please don't hang up. I beg you for everything you hold dear, leave Rafael. He will never be able to be happy knowing he left a child abandoned in Peru and me alone after he was the only man in my life. Knowing the shame I have to endure today because of him. Is that what you want for him? A life in darkness, knowing he could never walk with his head held high because of the cowardice he showed to me and his child. I am going to have a son, and I will name him Rafael like his father, even though his father abandoned him because of you. I ask you to reconsider, to return to Lima, to let him be close to his son. Let him be a father to this child who is not to blame for our mistakes. Please, Isabella, I beg you, do it. I ask you, as a mother, not to let my child grow up without a father. And if it is true that you love Rafael, don't allow him to stain his name, but above all, to create a wound in his heart that will never heal."

After the call ended, I sat on my bed with a heavy heart, my eyes clouded by the tears that had flowed during the call. I couldn't let Rafael be separated from that child who was innocent of everything. I myself had three daughters, two of whom had their father taken away by life. I knew well what they had suffered, and for that reason, I couldn't allow myself to make a decision that would lead another child to grow up away from his father.

The decision I will make next will turn my destiny around completely, for which I don't think I am prepared. But it won't be the first time something like this happens to me; I am starting to gain experience in living without a man by my side.

I believe I am well-prepared to face this pain, while I don't think María del Carmen is. I know I must think of myself, but the idea of causing her that harm, knowing she won't be able to overcome it, eats away at my soul.

I love Rafael as I have never loved anyone in this world before. I even know that after feeling so strongly for him, it will be impossible for me to love like this again. But I can't be blind. I have to accept that, even though I didn't want to see it before, Rafael has lied to me all these years we've been together, even from the first day we met. Knowing he had another woman in his life, he wasn't able to tell me and presented himself as a man without commitments, totally free, which was not true, and that is a fact I can no longer overlook. Although now he is calm, far from all that story, at some point, he has to return to face it.

But the most important reason for making this decision is that, from an early age, I learned that to love is, above all, to bring peace. I learned it by watching my grandparents love each other until their last days; my parents always respected and cared for each other.

Today, I have to accept with resignation that with Rafael, I will never be able to feel that peace, as with his lies, he made sure to steal my tranquility.

IX. The Turns Life Took

October 4, 2020

We've had some wonderful news lately. It started with a call from Mathi, my cousin, who told me he would be arriving in a week. To avoid any complications with COVID-19, he will go directly from the plane to a hotel for the first few days, get the necessary tests done, and once he has negative results, I will pick him up and take him to the rented house, where he will surprise everyone. I'm excited to plan this entire reunion, and I hope everything goes as planned. It will be a huge joy for everyone because we've been longing to hug him since we heard he overcame the challenging time during his hospitalization.

Later, Jane called to give me wonderful news: she and her husband wanted to ask me if I would like to be the godmother of the baby girl they are expecting around the end of November. Of course, I told them nothing would flatter me more than having that title; how could I not be the godmother of the daughter of someone who is more than a friend to me, a sister?

I took the opportunity to tell Jane about my trip to the Keys with Salomón. Honestly, I hadn't dared to talk to anyone about it. I suppose things happened as I thought they would, even though I tried to lie to myself by saying they wouldn't.

I explained to Jane in detail what happened that weekend, starting with how beautiful the city of Florida was. I also told her about the long walks full of laughter we took around downtown, bringing Mr. Marlei with us wherever we could. We were surprised that in Key West, it seemed like the coronavirus didn't exist, as there were people everywhere enjoying the restaurants and bars without much concern. While some nighttime entertainment places were closed, the majority were operating almost normally, which felt a bit strange. However, we maintained our precautions to protect ourselves from any unnecessary contagion by wearing masks, practicing social distancing, washing our hands constantly, and using hand sanitizer, among other measures we could take as much as possible.

Returning to what happened with Salomón, the first night after dinner, we decided to open a bottle of wine while we brought out some board games that came with the motorhome he rented. We were having a lot of fun, and without realizing it, we had already opened the second bottle of wine. We ended the evening playing cards, drinking wine, and talking about a thousand different things that jumped from topic to topic without any particular order; we just went with the flow of the conversation. After finishing the second bottle, we decided to stop the games and go to bed since we were already tired from the trip from home to the Keys, which took us a little over four hours due to the stops we had to make for Mr. Marlei to do his business.

We said goodnight, and each went to our room. When I was about to lie down, I accidentally tripped over a wire sticking out of the floor, making a loud noise that caught Salomón's attention. He ran to check if everything was okay in my room, and when he entered, he saw that I had a medium cut on my hand that was bleeding. In less than a second, he had the first aid kit open and had already laid out everything he needed to treat my wound on the bed. He carried me there and laid me down to start the treatment. At that moment, I remembered that Salomón was a doctor; with the games, laughter, walk, and wine, I had forgotten for a moment.

He meticulously cleaned and treated my wound with such tenderness that it deeply moved me. I don't know if it was the wine or a sincere reaction that led me to seek his lips with mine to kiss him. This kiss was very different from the first one we shared, as in this one, I felt my skin burn, and his hands on my hips were asking permission to undress me. I, on the other hand, didn't ask for any permission to do the same. We made love all night with vigor; there were plenty of kisses, caresses, and passion until the first rays of light came, announcing it was time to end the night, and we fell exhausted.

The next night, something similar happened with Salomón, but this time without the wine, so I felt it more. I must confess that I liked it, although I spent the entire weekend struggling with guilt, thinking that maybe it was too soon for me after having Javier in my life for the last few years. However, as I mentioned to Jane, it seems this struggle in my heart only happened in the mornings because when night came, it dissolved between Salomón's kisses and caresses.

I returned home with more doubts than I had when I left.

* * *

January 4, 1964

Today, I saw Rafael after almost six months of not letting him see me. While it is true that he has not stopped coming to see Paloma, I have tried all this time not to cross paths with him during his visits. But today, since it is Palomita's first birthday, I couldn't avoid the encounter any longer.

It happened that, although I had not planned to do anything special for Paloma, as I consider she is still too young to understand what is happening and the reason for the celebration, her father, along with my daughter Alba, organized a special dinner to honor her little sister. Alba was the most excited about the entire process, so I couldn't refuse to participate in all the preparations. I didn't want my Alba to feel saddened by my lack of enthusiasm.

My daughters have a lot of affection for Rafael, and that tears my heart apart. They always ask me why we came back from Chile; worse still, they question why he no longer lives with us. In their eyes, Rafael is a wonderful person. I never know how to explain what happened; all I can do is change the subject, trying to hide my sorrow. For Alondra, my stammered answers after each question about the subject may be more believable. However, I sense that Alba understands that something is wrong between Rafael and me, so she asks less and even helps me avoid Alondra's questions about it.

For dinner, Rafael arranged for María, the lady who always prepared special meals for us, to make arroz con pollo, Alba's favorite dish, considering the birthday girl was still too young to decide what she wanted for dinner on her day. He also bought some special birthday decorations, which he hung with the girls in the living room and dining room to make the atmosphere more festive. Lastly, he ordered a strawberry cake with dulce de leche, Alondra's favorite, to please both of them with their requests.

After dinner, Rafael stayed to help us clear the table and tidy up the house after the celebration, even though we had no other guests besides those who lived in the house, including Ana, who still faithfully stays by my side. Everything was normal until I suddenly heard Alba telling Alondra that it was late and they had to go to bed, so Ana took them by the hand to help them get to sleep. I didn't realize when we were left alone, but it happened. We were in the living room, picking up the last decorations without speaking but exchanging glances whenever we could, not considering the consequences of what that would entail.

Rafael and I made love that night, as we always had as if nothing had happened between us, as if he were still my husband, even though I knew he was no longer mine. He was not mine in body, but his soul was still mine. When the moment of madness passed, I asked Rafael to leave my house; that when he comes to visit Paloma, he should continue doing so as he has been, without seeking me out, without having any contact with me; that he should coordinate everything with Ana as always; for me, he no longer existed. I made it clear that what had just happened was just a slip on my part, but it meant nothing.

Remembering Rafael's face while I said all this, I feel a lump in my throat, and my breath shortens as if that lie had gotten stuck in its path from my chest to my mouth. When Rafael left, the door closed, and I collapsed behind it, feeling that, along with him, my soul was leaving.

While I felt like dying, perhaps in an attempt to catch my breath, I forced myself to remember what happened after deciding to return from Chile with my daughters a few days after having that conversation with María del Carmen and definitively ending my relationship with Rafael, knowing he continued his life with her. Although it is true, from what I have heard, they do not live in the same house, but they see each other a lot, even sharing as a family in different social events. I also know that the baby was born and that, as she told me, she named him Rafael. Deep down, I am glad to hear that it is a healthy baby and that my ex-husband adores him as I assumed he would when he saw him in his arms. The child is not to blame for anything, and that is why I left Rafael, so he could be close to his son, just as is happening. I trust that my decision to leave who was then my husband and return to Peru was the right one.

February 23, 1965

What a beautiful celebration I managed to organize for Alba's twelfth birthday. I see her gradually becoming a beautiful young woman, full of virtues that astonish and admire me. She has been and is my support for everything, the one who keeps my feet firmly on the ground without even realizing it. My princess has a wonderful heart for which I am infinitely grateful every day.

For her birthday, in addition to the charming celebration we organized, we gifted her a spot in ballet classes at the San Marcos Ballet School. We know of her love for this art and how much she wanted to attend these classes. I write in the plural because Rafael was involved in getting this gift. Knowing Alba's desire, he spoke with a cousin close to the school's administration and thus managed to enroll her in classes throughout the year. Alba cried with happiness when she found out about this special gift, the cherry on top to end her celebration day for her twelve springs.

Regarding Rafael, I had managed the situation with his visits to the house and my way of avoiding him very well. But as I wrote a couple of months ago, last Christmas, I was forced to attend his visit since Ana had the day off, so I had to wait for Rafael to bring Paloma, whom he had taken to spend the day with him and his parents to celebrate the holidays. It happened that once again, I succumbed to his arms, surrendering completely to him as we had almost a year ago on our daughter's first birthday. It happened, and once again, I repeated the speech that he shouldn't seek me out, that it wouldn't happen again, although inside, I begged him to seek me, to insist a thousand more times, for I would say yes, those thousand times.

Returning to the present day, and since Rafael helped arrange the special gift for Alba, I couldn't refuse his attendance at the birthday party we organized for her.

Rafael, as always, was impeccable from head to toe; it seemed he had dressed to commemorate an important event, which, of course, for me, it was. I hadn't seen him since last Christmas when we parted without even looking at each other after spending the night together in my bed.

I wore a simple but pleasant dress that, by the way, fit me very well, accentuating the curves of my body and leaving my shoulders bare. I suppose I chose it to know he would attend the celebration, though I don't want to admit it.

When we greeted each other, we couldn't avoid scanning each other with our eyes; we have always had that unique way of connecting without saying a word. At the end of the party, we were left alone again, but this time, we knew what would happen; this time, we didn't try to hide by cleaning or picking up anything: we went straight to my room, where we tore off each other's clothes as best we could and made love.

When we finished, I asked Rafael not to speak, not to say anything.

"Rafael, just gather your things and leave."

"I love you, Bella. Nothing and no one will change that." He replied as he walked to the door before leaving.

April 8, 1965

This morning, when I passed by Mr. Jorge's bakery, which I often visit, I stopped to listen to a somewhat uneasy conversation that a small group of customers were having at that moment. I was drawn to their discussion when they mentioned that, according to some news outlets, a rebel movement was rising in the countryside, seeking to destabilize the government of the current president as they disagreed with his administration. Some of these rebels were using violence in their demonstrations, which concerned them.

At that moment, paying more attention to the conversation than to where I was going, I stumbled into a young man about six or seven years younger than me, spilling all my purchases on top of him.

The young man was of average height, neither tall nor short, but he had a rather handsome face, highlighted by fine features and a sweet gaze. He was very well dressed and seemed to be in no hurry. He didn't complain about what I had done to his suit; on the contrary, he took the time to help me gather everything scattered on the ground without saying a word. Worried about having dirtied his clothes, I anxiously tried to ask if I could help shake off the breadcrumbs still clinging to his jacket, but the young man paid no attention.

"I'm sorry." That was all I could manage to say.

"There's no need to worry, beautiful; everything is fine. My name is Eduardo. It's been a pleasure."

May 14, 1965

"Good morning, beautiful. What a pleasure to find you here. I hope you won't greet me with bread on top today." Eduardo cheerfully welcomed me from behind.

"Hello, how are you? Sorry again for what happened that day; I was distracted."

"Don't worry, beautiful. I barely remember what happened. The only thing I remember in detail is your face and your voice. Do you come here often?

"Yes, I live nearby. I often come to shop at this store. How about you?"

"Well, I recently returned from a long trip. For now, I'm staying with my mother. She lives close by, so when time allows, I help her with her shopping, so she doesn't have to carry the bags in the street. She's an older lady, and with this summer heat that still refuses to leave, it's too much for her."

"I'm glad you look after your mother. Well, I have to go; if I linger too long, the day will be too short for all the tasks I have pending."

"Let me accompany you, please. Just as I don't allow my mother to carry the shopping bags, I wouldn't let you do it either; besides, you might stumble into someone and end up spilling your groceries on them like you did with me," he said, laughing.

"It's not necessary, really. I like to walk. I take that moment of the day to think."

"I won't interrupt those thoughts; I just want to help carry the bags. Besides, you haven't told me your name. I'd like to know the name of the pretty girl who covered my clothes with bread and cheese a couple of weeks ago."

"My name is Isabella Martini. Sorry for my lack of manners in not introducing myself; I've been a bit distracted these days. My daughters recently started school, and I'm still getting used to the routine."

"You have daughters, wow... I didn't think you were married with children. You look incredibly young."

"I'm not married; I'm a widow with three daughters. Your words flatter me, saying I look young, although I'm not as young as you think. In fact, you look much younger than me. How old are you?"

"I'm twenty-nine, but I'll be thirty in a few months."

August 17, 1965

Since May 14, when I met Eduardo, he hasn't stopped visiting me. He has become not only an emotional support but also a physical one, important to me at home. Despite my efforts to manage as a single woman, there are moments when I greatly enjoy his help. For example, a few days ago, while I was doing a small remodel in the girls' room, his strength and youthful vigor were vital to avoid Ana and me breaking our backs moving and carrying everything alone. Eduardo is also a very pleasant person. You can talk about everything with him, even trivial topics that some other men consider solely for women. I enjoy listening to him speak; he is very educated and cultured for his age. The age difference between us does not seem to be a barrier to the beautiful complicity that has grown between Eduardo and me.

A few days ago, he introduced me to his best friend, a guy who could be the same age as Eduardo, although not as educated and cultured as he is. However, his presence is quite striking. José, that's

Eduardo's friend's name, is a tall, dark-skinned guy with a broad back, sunburned brown hair, a soft but firm voice, large eyes, and thick eyebrows. He seems to be from a humble economic background, judging by the way he dressed the day we met, or at least that was the impression he gave me.

I think I haven't mentioned that the day Eduardo first accompanied me home, he stole a kiss when we said goodbye. It was an innocent kiss, like teenagers, where he just touched his lips to mine for a few seconds. Then he said "goodbye" and almost ran off.

In the following days, there were some other kisses. I must admit that the last kisses have ceased to be so innocent and have turned into more feverish exchanges, occasionally accompanied by caresses, but the kisses do not lead to any other kind of encounter.

At times, this confuses me. I always suspected that men were not known for controlling their sexual impulses, but Eduardo does not seem to be one of those; he controls himself very well. Deep down, I think it is better that things happen this way, as I wouldn't want to regret anything later.

Eduardo visited me today, as usual, in the late afternoon. He surprised me by proposing that we start a relationship together. I didn't know what to answer. He even mentioned that he thinks we could try living together to see if being a couple works. He said that in his travels through Europe, he met couples who lived together without getting married and got along great, loving each other without the tedious routine that falls upon one when married. I still don't know how to respond to his proposal. It has left me stunned, as I didn't even remotely intend to have a relationship with anyone at this moment, much less a romance of the kind Eduardo proposes.

December 10, 1965

We began preparing for the holidays at home. With three little ones around, I can't help but celebrate Christmas as it should be, just as we always did when my grandparents and parents were alive.

The turkey at Christmas Eve dinner is a must. I'll stuff it with apples and raisins, just as my father liked, and use my grandmother's recipe for mashed potatoes with garlic and rosemary. For dessert, perhaps an apple or strawberry pie.

Alba is grown up and beautiful. She is the most enthusiastic about holiday preparations. She handles the shopping lists and always finds ways to decorate the house for the occasion so that the festive atmosphere can be felt in our home. Although she is about to turn thirteen, she still holds on to a child's excitement, which brings me immense joy to see her with her younger sisters, moving things around to fit her decoration plan for this Christmas.

Alondra, on the other hand, is more relaxed and goes along with whatever her older sister suggests. At times, it even seems to me that she doesn't enjoy the tasks her sister assigns her, especially when it comes to cleaning, but she doesn't object much. She knows her sister is quite adamant when she has something in mind and prefers to avoid upsetting her by refusing or complaining.

Paloma, for her part, is already quite talkative. She has us all wrapped around her finger, walking confidently around the house, mimicking everything her older sisters do or say, and making us smile with her antics, especially her father, who is utterly smitten with her.

Speaking of Rafael, I wanted to write a bit about him. Today, I saw him again after the last time, on Alba's twelfth birthday, when we ended up in bed, disregarding everything that had happened between us before.

Rafael looked incredibly good, as always, with that distinctive presence. He was dressed casually but still elegant. He came to see Paloma because he won't be in Lima for the Christmas holidays this year and wanted our daughter to see her grandparents for a few hours.

A few days ago, I heard that María del Carmen, his current partner and the mother of his child, was apparently pregnant again, only a few months along. This news didn't surprise me, even though Rafael always made it seem like he wasn't serious with anyone, that his relationship with María del Carmen was just a formality for their child's sake, who is almost the same age as Paloma. However, with the news of the new pregnancy, there was no doubt that he did have a relationship with her, even if he denied it, and that the baby María del Carmen was expecting was indeed Rafael's.

At first, I thought about confronting him about his lie, but I quickly realized I had no right to do so. Instead, I decided to say something else when I saw him appear at my living room door looking for our daughter.

"Hello, Rafael. What time will you bring Paloma back?"

"Hello, Bella. How are you? From what I see, I can say you're doing well. Yellow looks beautiful on you; I've always said so."

"Thank you, Rafael. I must say you look good too. It must be the air that comes with a new baby on the way for your family. Let me congratulate you on that. A child is always a blessing."

"Uh... well, I... Rafael began to respond, unable to form words; he was visibly surprised by what he had just heard."

"No, you don't have to say anything; don't worry. My congratulations are sincere. I hope María del Carmen and you are happy with the arrival of your new baby. I truly wish you all the best in the home you have formed."

"I, on the other hand, Bella, cannot say the same."

"I don't understand what you mean, Rafael."

"I don't congratulate your decision to start a relationship with that man you've been bringing into your house without hesitation, a man you barely know and have no idea who he is or what he wants from you. I know you are seeing Eduardo, and you don't even know where he came from, right? It would be wise to be concerned

188

about what kind of person he is, especially if you're going to let him into your home and share your daughters' time with him."

"Rafael! I won't allow you to come to my house and judge my decisions, much less question my daughters' well-being by insinuating that I don't care for them properly. I will not tolerate such disrespect, especially from someone who has no moral authority to speak. This is the first and last time you will address any matter of my private life that only concerns me. Your opinions on my life are unwelcome."

It was at that moment, as if from heaven, Paloma appeared, holding Ana's hand. Ana had dressed and styled her beautifully to go out with her father.

Paloma came bouncing with joy. As soon as she saw her father's figure, she ran to hug him, and Rafael's face immediately changed upon seeing his little girl. I had no choice but to join in Paloma's happiness, kiss her goodbye, and watch her leave with Rafael. The topic of Eduardo between us ended there.

When Paloma returned, Rafael simply said to me:

"Goodbye, Isabella. When I return from my trip, I will come to see Paloma. In her suitcase, I left Christmas gifts for her and her sisters. Please give the presents to the girls on Christmas Eve. Thank you."

X. The Painful Truth

* * *

January 4, 1966

To me, it feels like just yesterday that we rushed to the hospital after my water broke while I was showering. I remember screaming in the bathroom for Rafael to come help me when I realized it was time. Exactly three years have passed since then, and today we celebrate another year of my beloved Paloma's life, the girl who came into our lives as a result of an immense love that now I can only remember with nostalgia, as it feels distant.

Once again, and as has become customary at home, Alba took charge of organizing the celebration for the baby of the family. She spent the entire morning running up and down with the preparations for Paloma's party, which, by the way, was magnificent.

We invited a couple of Alba and Alondra's schoolmates since Paloma still doesn't go to school and, therefore, doesn't have friends her age. However, she has a fun time when her older sisters'

191

friends come over to play. The girls had a wonderful time with games, music, food, and laughter.

When it was time to sing Happy Birthday, we were pleasantly surprised by the beautiful cake Rafael had ordered for his little girl from the new bakery on Jirón de la Unión, where many people in Lima are now ordering their cakes for special occasions.

At the end of the celebration, when all the guests had left and even the girls were getting ready for bed, Rafael asked me to spare a few minutes to talk alone. At first, I refused because it seemed to me that this was becoming a recurrent issue for us since I noticed that whenever we had the chance to see each other under the pretense of discussing something important about our daughter, we ended up making love. This time, I wouldn't allow it, not only because I didn't want to fall into that trap anymore but also because I was no longer alone; I now had Eduardo in my life, to whom I owed respect.

After much insistence from Rafael, I agreed to talk, but not before warning him that it would only be a short conversation since Eduardo was waiting for the party to end so he could. I lied.

"Bella, that's what exactly I wanted to talk about. I know that the last time we touched on this subject, things didn't turn out well, but I'd like to know what your plans are with that man, not because I selfishly don't want you to be happy or have someone by your side. Please don't think that way. My concern is solely for the girls but mainly for my daughter, whom I am obligated to look after. I'd like to know what your intentions are with him and how far you plan to go with all this."

"Rafael, Eduardo, and I are going to move in together in a few weeks; he's going to come live with us. We're finalizing the details. For now, we don't plan to get married, but we will start living together with a view to an upcoming wedding. Regarding this, I don't think I need to give you more details than I'm giving you now. Lastly, I don't think you have anything to worry about; he is a decent person. I know his mother; she holds me in high regard and respects me, so you have nothing to fear. My daughters will always be cared for by me and with Ana's company, as we have been doing until now. I appreciate your concern, but I repeat: there's nothing to worry about. Regarding Paloma, you can come for her whenever you like; we will maintain the routine you've had with our daughter until now. Eduardo is informed and agrees with everything; what I do ask is that if our meetings have been few but have happened until now, from today, they should be minimal, as I wouldn't want to make my partner uncomfortable, much less have our conversations lead to misunderstandings. I hope you understand."

"Bella, how can you tell me all that? How can you suddenly tell me that a man is going to move into your house and that we won't even be able to talk? Don't you feel any pity for me at all? You're breaking my heart into a thousand pieces, and it doesn't affect you at all. You can't do this."

"Calm down, Rafael. Don't raise your voice in my house; the girls are already going to bed. I don't want to disturb their sleep. Moreover, how can you have the nerve to say all that when you are the one who, since we met, has never had any pity for me at all? You were the one who broke my heart and never cared. You never picked up the pieces of my heart or my life after destroying it, not just once, but many times, with each of your lies and deceit. Authority, authority, do you ask me why I don't feel pity for you?"

"Bella, don't say that. You know very well that I love you and have never stopped loving you and never will. Don't compare yourself to me; my case is different. It's not something I sought but something imposed on me, and I haven't been able to escape out of cowardice. I even sought your support to take that step, but you left me halfway, knowing that without you, I couldn't advance further in that process. We had a deal, Bella; we'd do everything right in Chile, and you threw everything away, leaving me with no ground to stand on. What did you want me to do?"

"I wanted you not to lie to me. I wanted to know love, but the good kind, the beautiful kind, the kind I knew from my grandparents and my parents, the love that brings peace, which helps you grow and that matures over the years. That's what I wanted, but it seemed too much to ask from you. You could never give me that, and you never will because you're selfish, Rafael; you only seek your own well-being without caring who you drag along the way. I don't blame you, you know? I've learned to forgive you."

"Maybe the way your parents raised you made you believe it was normal to love like that, but it's not. I was raised differently, and I want to pass on those values to my daughters; I want them to see me as an example when they grow up. Now, please leave. You know what you wanted to know; we have nothing more to talk about. Thanks for helping with Paloma's celebration. For any additional details, you know you can talk to Ana from now on."

"Isabella, no! I'm not going to end the conversation here. Or don't you realize it's always like this with you? You don't like talking about our issues; you always run away from them. You think you're very mature, but you're not when it comes to talking about your feelings. What are you afraid of? That we might end up making love again? Because that's what we do when we're together—we make love. Rafael furiously replied while grabbing my arms to pull me close to his body."

"Nothing you say or do will change my mind, Rafael. Eduardo will come to live with me, and we'll start a new life, forming a home for the five of us, a home that could have been yours but will never be."

We ended up making love again. That night was a mixture of rage and pain for both of us. We didn't want to separate our bodies because we knew very well that once we did, we would return to reality, a reality that was not favorable to us and that, on the contrary, caused us anguish. When we finally parted, it was almost midnight, so hurriedly, I asked Rafael to leave quietly; I didn't want to wake the girls or Ana.

I'll leave the diary here because tomorrow awaits a long day. I have to rest; I hope I can after everything that has happened today.

May 8, 1966

Life keeps tangling me in its web, and at times it feels suffocating. Today has been no exception.

What I feel is a mix of pain and pity. The love story I built like a house of cards has collapsed, supported only by my desire to be loved. I just now realized that I was the only one who believed in the story with Eduardo since even his mother couldn't fully process that he and I were more than friends.

Now I understand why, after almost a year of knowing Eduardo, we only made love once. It was the night he moved in. We did it almost at my insistence; in that act, Eduardo was very clumsy, far different from what I had imagined it would be. I attributed his incompetence to his youth, thinking that the five-year age difference between us could be felt in that aspect. I now know that was just an excuse on my part not to see what I already suspected and now see without disguise.

It happened this afternoon when realizing I had forgotten the book I was reading at Eduardo's mother's house. I decided to stop by to retrieve it and continue reading in my free time. Additionally, I had to pick up a pending order from the store, which was close to her house. When I arrived, I found the front door not fully closed, which surprised me a bit, but I entered directly. Upon entering, I encountered an image I hadn't been able to erase from my mind all day and doubt I ever will: I saw Eduardo in the arms of his friend José, with whom he was kissing passionately. Between kisses, he told him to forgive him, that he loved him, and to give him more time. José, the friend I had met months ago in that same house, whom his mother also knew and who I can now unequivocally affirm there were things between her son and José that couldn't be considered just friendship. That boy, who at first glance seemed simple, dressed humbly, with an introverted personality and a soft but determined voice, was kissing my current partner with a passion I had never been able to awaken in him before.

In my thoughts, I could imagine a thousand things about the lack of enthusiasm I saw in Eduardo towards me as a romantic partner. I even came to believe that I wasn't a good enough lover the first and only time we slept together. I thought at times that maybe Eduardo might have a lover who was more uninhibited in bed, but I quickly dismissed that idea since he spent most of his time with me or his mother, so the idea of a lover left my mind as quickly as it appeared.

Now, this monster starts to have feet and a head; this is the moment I decipher the ghost that haunted me regarding my relationship.

Life once again shows me its ugliest face, one I was once again unprepared for. I see my dreams of a stable home fading, slipping away without being able to do anything about it, as I understand it's not in my hands to change this tyrannical fate.

Eduardo, realizing my presence in the room, dropped what he had in his hand to push José, who fell to the floor with such force that he broke the coffee table on his way down. I ran to help José, who was still in shock over what had just happened.

"Bella, please, let me explain everything. Eduardo said as he ran to help José as well."

"Eduardo, I think there's a lot to talk about, but I don't think this is the place or the time. What I just saw is clear enough for me. However, we do need to talk and discuss what will happen from now on, but please give me time to process all this."

"It's better if I leave," José said, hurt from the fall and trying to recover not only from the pain but also from the shock.

"Don't go, José. Stay with Eduardo; keep him company. I'm the one who's leaving; I have to continue with my routine. Don't worry. What I just saw only concerns the three of us, and I won't say anything to anyone or do anything against you. Eduardo, I just ask that you don't come home for now; wait for me to reach out to you. Give me a few days to do so. I'll tell the girls that your mother is sick, and you'll be taking care of her while she recovers. Then, I hope you'll tell me the truth about all this; it's the only thing you can't deny me, the truth."

June 1, 1966

Today, I managed to gather the strength to talk to Eduardo about what I saw at his house. He, for his part, respected what we agreed on and didn't seek me out in the following days, giving me time to reflect on everything I went through at that moment. However, I believe that even a thousand years wouldn't have been enough for me to process all the information that was crossing my mind.

"Thank you for coming, Bella. Please sit down so we can be comfortable. Don't worry; we are alone."

"Eduardo, I don't know where to start this conversation, but what I do know is that, before we begin, I want to ask you for all the sincerity you can offer me about yourself. I want you to tell me who you are and where you want to go as much as you can."

"You have the right to know, Bella, and I am obliged to tell you. Don't worry. This afternoon, I will open my heart to you as I have never done before. I will tell you the truth, even if it hurts."

I learned many aspects of Eduardo's life that I could never have imagined, even in my wildest dreams. I learned how José came into his life; he confirmed that both, a couple of years ago, were part of one of those revolutionary groups that are now starting to be felt across Peru, that they even traveled together to Cuba as part of a committee that went to that country to prepare for the conflict that would start here a few years later, according to their plans. He also told me that it was during that trip that their relationship began.

Upon their return to Peru, the romantic relationship strengthened, shielded by the complicity of both being fighters for the revolution in the country, but little by little, the rumors of Eduardo's delicacy and the way they cared for and treated each other started to echo within the group they belonged to.

"You can't imagine everything we have been through, Bella. We are here by miracle. When the rumors started getting stronger, they didn't leave us alone. One night, several group members decided to find out what exactly united us, so they followed us after one of the usual meetings. It was then that they found out where we lived and that we lived together. They didn't like this at all, so they decided to take action. About thirteen people armed with sticks, cables, ropes, stones, and other things entered our house. They tied our hands and feet, tore our clothes, and started beating us with everything they could while hurling offensive words at us about our sexual preferences. I took the worst part because I couldn't bear to see them torturing José's body and face, so I responded to their insults to provoke them into taking their anger out on me, and they did so without hesitation. After almost forty minutes of beatings and insults, one of them shouted, "Stop, he's dead!" upon noticing that I could no longer hold my head up. It was then that they began to leave the house, but not before attempting to set it on fire. A neighbor, our friend, saw what had happened but couldn't do anything but wait, praying for them to leave. Once she confirmed they had left, she entered the house, which was starting to burn, and dragged José's and my bodies out as best she could. If it weren't for her, we wouldn't be alive today.

Bella, those men didn't kill us physically that night, but they killed our souls. We didn't know what humans were capable of doing to one another just because they believed their way of thinking or being was the only valid one. We understood that night that we couldn't love each other; we tried to separate many times, but it was impossible. Even you are a witness to the fact that I tried to build a life with you, a family, a home, but I failed, Bella."

"What happened to those people who broke into your house?"

"Nothing happened. We didn't say anything. How could we report something like that? What would we say about our romance? That we were queers? So that then other people like them would come to do the same, and who knows if there would be a miracle to save us! Besides, calling the police would have been putting a noose around our necks. Remember, we were part of an illegal group; I was aware that pulling one thread would unravel everything."

"So, what did you two do?"

"The best we could do at that moment: we fled. We went to Bolivia for almost a year, where we worked at anything we could to support ourselves while we waited for things to calm down here in Peru. But my mother got sick, and as you know, I am her only child. I couldn't leave her alone, so I returned to see her. I managed to contact close family friends living in La Paz, who helped me with a loan and a place to stay while I organized my return. José couldn't come back to me because my mother didn't know about him then, and being as sick as she was, it was better not to give her additional problems. Later, I was able to send the necessary money for José to return to Peru, but not before paying all our debts in Bolivia."

"Does your mother know about your relationship with José?"

"My mother and I have never spoken openly. However, she knows me very well. I know she senses that José and I love each other, but her religion and beliefs don't allow her to sit down and talk to me about it. I know life hasn't been entirely kind to you, Bella, but it hasn't been for me either. You can imagine what it's like to grow up knowing that someone else lives inside you. I have never felt free in my own body or mind. I have always had to act, playing the role of someone far from being me. When I was a child, between seven and eight years old, I saw a classmate showering in the school bathroom after sports. I watched him for several minutes, unable to take my eyes off him; from that night on, I daydreamed about that boy and didn't understand why. Today, I know that day I awoke the monster that had been asleep, the one that now haunts me, preventing me from being what everyone wants me to be: a "normal" man."

June 4, 1966

As I was preparing to celebrate my thirty-fifth birthday with my little ones and Ana, Rafael arrived at the house with the cake in hand. According to him, Alba had called him, worried because

Eduardo hadn't come home for several weeks and she had no one to ask to fetch a cake from my favorite bakery to wait until midnight together at a dinner that, as always, she had prepared with so much care for me.

The dinner was delightful. Ana outdid herself with the food, which turned out very tasty. Rafael brought a bottle of white wine that brought back wonderful memories of dinners at home when my grandparents and parents were alive. Of course, the cake was not missing at the end of the meal.

The girls, with Rafael's help, gave me a beautiful bouquet of twenty-four white roses after singing Happy Birthday to me. At the end of the dinner, I went to the kitchen to get the vase to place them. It didn't take more than ten minutes, and when I came out with the flowers ready to adorn the table, the girls and Ana had already left to start organizing their beds to rest. Rafael, on the other hand, was waiting for me at the table with the wine glasses served.

"Bella, you don't turn thirty-five every day. Besides, the wine I brought is Italian, as you like. I had it ordered months ago, waiting for the special moment to open it; the moment is today. Remember that I also turn years; both of us turn thirty-five today. Have a glass with me as a gift."

I won't go into additional details about what happened that night, only that we ended up sleeping together once again, and once again, I swore I wouldn't do it again, no longer for María del

Carmen, nor for Eduardo; it wasn't for anyone else but myself. I wouldn't give myself to Rafael anymore because he didn't deserve it. He didn't deserve my caresses or my kisses, my time or my warmth, and my body and much less my soul, and I didn't deserve to feel how I felt when he left, when he returned to his life with his family while I stayed with his scent lingering, his scent of wood and honey in the room, in the bed, in my hair, but most of all in my heart.

August 19, 1966

"Eduardo, hi. It's Bella. I need you to come to my house; we need to talk. It's urgent."

"Hi, Bella, sure, tell me the time, and I'll be there."

"Come right now; it's urgent. Let's take advantage of the fact that the girls are at school, and Ana has gone to the market with Paloma to get some things."

"Wait for me. I'll throw something on and head to your house."

Minutes later, Eduardo arrived.

"Eduardo, come in. Please sit down. I need to talk to you about what you mentioned the other day that you were planning to do with José."

"You mean the trip to the United States?"

"Yes, that. Tell me exactly what you have planned and what possibilities you have of settling in that country. Who is the person who is going to help you when you get there? Tell me everything you can."

"But, Bella, why are you so interested in this now if, when I told you that José and I had been mulling over that idea, you responded that we were crazy?"

"Things are different now, Eduardo. I think I was hasty in responding to you that afternoon when you suggested we all go to the United States. I've been thinking things over these past few days, and I see that the idea isn't entirely crazy; on the contrary, maybe it's the change my life has been screaming at me to take."

"I can't believe what you're telling me now. What great news! You know I'd love for you and the girls to come with us. We can start a whole new life far from here. I've made a lot of progress in the arrangements. Let me give you the details so you can see the plan is foolproof."

"Before you give me more information, I want to tell you something, Eduardo. I'm pregnant. I realized a few days ago that I hadn't had my period for a little over two months. With all the craziness that's happened these days, I had overlooked that detail. As soon as I realized it, I ran to the doctor, who confirmed that I was expecting a baby. I'm pregnant, and the baby is Rafael's. Neither he nor anyone else can know; we will say the baby is yours, and we're moving to America together, and that you have a job offer there that you can't refuse, so we will plan our departure as soon as possible. We will also say that José is going with us, as he has also been hired by the same company that hired you.

Once we get to the United States, we'll see how things develop and the direction each of us will take. Eduardo, I want it to be clear that saying we're going together is just to avoid raising suspicions about my pregnancy, nothing more. You know you have to help me with this. You will, right?"

"Bella, I don't know what to say. I wasn't expecting any of this."

"Eduardo, now is not the time to stop and think about anything else; what's done is done. For now, let's not get tangled up in additional issues and get the project going as soon as possible. Give me the details of what you've found out so we can see what else we need. Let's find dates and shape the plan as soon as possible. I don't want my pregnancy to show before we get to the United States."

* * *

November 16, 2020

It has been eight months since this whole COVID-19 pandemic madness broke out around the world. While we all gradually adjust to our daily routine, which was once enjoyed live and in person, like simply going to a doctor's appointment or school for the children, many people, including myself, have started to let our guard down regarding the concern about the disease, as most of us by now have already contracted the virus at some point and managed to overcome it. There are also those who have not yet been infected or those who have been left with severe side effects after having had the coronavirus, not to mention those who have lost loved ones infected with the virus.

On the other hand, I don't know if things in my life are starting to settle down or if everything is falling apart; I can do nothing about it. Personally, I managed to put an end to my relationship with Javier. I spoke with him calmly, and we both concluded that our relationship had no future. I can't help but mention here that I didn't expect Javier's positive reaction to this matter. I thought he would have a tough time ending our love bond; however, he accepted my proposal to leave things as they were. Then I found out from Jane that, the day after our conversation, Javier introduced his new partner on his social media with a photo and the following note: "Thank you, my love, for making my gray pandemic days bearable. Without you by my side these months, I wouldn't have been able to overcome many things I had to go through."

Deep down in my heart, I felt at peace, and I can even say happy that Javier found someone to enjoy life with, perhaps because it freed me from guilt or because I genuinely loved him a lot.

Regarding Salomón, since we went to the Keys in June, we have seen each other quite often, mostly at his house, where we share meals, as well as kisses and caresses that always end up in his bed, making me feel loved; his way of making love is really that: LOVE. However, I can't seem to reconcile with that situation, as every time I return home after an encounter with him, Bella's diary comes to mind, the moment she describes what she experiences when Rafael leaves home after having slept with him. I put myself in her shoes and shared with her that distress, that pain from years ago.

As if all these changes weren't enough, I also have to add that now I can't stop thinking about everything I've come to discover by reading my grandmother's diary. Although I still have several pages to finish, I consider that I am at the exact moment Bella referred to when she said, "It's not time to say much about the diary, Perla. As you read it, you will understand why I'm telling you this. You will know yourself when you need to find me to talk about what you're going to read there. Also, I want you to know that, from the day I decided that it would be you who read it and made it known, I voluntarily accepted everything that entailed, meaning what it would imply for the fate of this family. Look for me to talk about it when your inner self tells you it's time; meanwhile, keep reading."

* * *

October 18, 1966

"Hello, Bella. Sorry to come to your house unannounced, but I was excited. I wanted to tell you that I already have the tickets in hand for our trip to New York. Everything is going as we planned."

"Don't worry, Eduardo, you can come whenever you want. We've already talked about this. We even mentioned that the more they see you around here, the better. Sit down. I'm finishing up the stew; join me for lunch so you can tell me everything.

We have the plane tickets with a departure date and no return date, marked for November 1 at four in the afternoon. The five of us will make the trip together, leaving from Jorge Chávez International Airport, which was inaugurated last year, and I haven't had the chance to visit yet. We will arrive at Miami City Airport, find a hotel to spend the night, and then head on a road trip by bus that will take us to New York; there, Eduardo's cousin will welcome us and settle us into our temporary home, which we have already rented for a month while we decide what to do next."

"Don't worry, Bella. My cousin has taken care of the house for our arrival, making sure it's comfortable, especially for the girls. We also have markets nearby to do our shopping and parks where they can spend some time. I want to remind you that the weather in New York is quite different from what we have here in Lima, especially in the winter, which is quite harsh there. In November, the weather suitcases get cold, so it would be good to keep this in mind when packing the suitcases. It's also important not to travel with too many things, as it will make it difficult to move around once we arrive in the United States.

In that country, there's everything, so if we need something, we can easily get it later. Let's try to bring only the essentials on the trip. Besides, my cousin has told me that she has managed to get the basic things we will need for the first days in the house, like beds, blankets, some cleaning supplies, and packaged foods like milk, rice, and sugar, which will help us survive until we get to know the area well enough to shop, as we get used to the neighborhood and the new routine."

"That's great, Eduardo. I'm glad we have someone's support in that city, so we won't be so alone, especially at the beginning, as you say, when everything will be new to us. I won't deny that I'm quite anxious about what we are about to experience. Although I have no doubt that life will be on my side this time, I can get through what lies ahead without much trouble. Don't get me wrong. It's not that I want things to be extremely easy. I just seek a little peace for myself and mainly for my little ones, who have endured all the vicissitudes with me and always with a smile, giving me the strength that often seemed to abandon me. Anyway, Eduardo, it's not the time for nostalgia; on the contrary, it's time to be braver and more determined than ever. A new life awaits us. Let's be ready."

"That's right, Bella. There are many reasons for us to be hopeful about this new stage. You have your beautiful daughters and also a new baby on the way. As for me, I'm seeking freedom. I want to allow myself to live in a country where no one knows me, where I don't have to pretend to be someone else, where I can be myself from day one, as I won't have to keep up appearances for anyone. I seek not only the freedom to love and be loved but also the freedom to feel as I truly am. People talked a lot about this with my cousin. She always tells me about the freedom people have in that city, where there isn't the same moral judgment as in Lima; there, people don't judge you by your appearance or where you live. My cousin says that America is the land of freedom. Recently, they even opened the doors to immigrants seeking diversity in their culture. The president enacted that law, and the citizens were happy. José and I are excited about the trip. I suppose deep down, we are eager to escape from everything we've lived through here in Peru. The only person I'll miss is my mother, but as soon as we settle in, she will come to visit me; she is the one who lent José and me the money to make this journey. My mother is an angel. I am grateful to her. I know she will suffer when we leave, but deep down, she knows it's the best for us, and that gives her peace."

XI. The End

November 24, 2020

"Good morning, Perla, dear. How did you wake up today?"

"Good morning, Bella. I was just thinking about you. Let's take advantage of the morning, which I have free, and talk. I must tell you that I'm almost finished with your second journal. You can imagine that I'm impressed by so much completely new information. I have many questions and need you to help clear them up."

"Of course, my dear. As I told you, I'm here for that. I was just waiting for you to reach the part of the story where you needed to come to me for help understanding it."

"Bella, before we begin, I want to know who, besides you and me, has read these journals before."

"No one else, Perla, only you."

"Does this mean that no one knows what you wrote there? No one knows the real reason you came to the United States, and that Dad is actually not Eduardo's son but Rafael's, so Aunt Paloma and he share the same father, and thus my dad has two more brothers in Peru. Does he have family there?"

"No one but me, Eduardo, and now you know about that."

"Bella, I don't want you to think I'm reproaching you for anything, but all this is hard for me to process. How did you not think Dad had the right to know who his father was and to meet him? You even told me that you found out Rafael died recently. What led you to hide that truth all this time, Bella? A truth that would change many things in my father's life, even in mine."

"Dear, I always did things thinking of the well-being of those involved at the time. Time, though you don't see it now because you're young, passes very quickly, and before you know it, forty or fifty years have passed. Then you think that if you've survived until then with the life you've been leading, why change it? That change could put our happiness at risk, and that's why it's hard to make that decision. That's what happened to me, dear. Everything in life has been so difficult for me. It was hard for me to come to this country, leaving everything in Peru, where I had a comfortable, calm life without rush. Coming here to start from scratch in a completely new city for everyone, not speaking the language, in a culture so different from Lima, without family, and with three girls and a baby in my belly, was quite complicated for me. I also had to add that I was fleeing from a painful truth, believing that I would forget everything here, or at least that's what I wanted to think when I left escaping in 1966."

"Bella, I don't intend to judge or criticize any of your decisions from that time or now; on the contrary, what I want is to understand what happened and why now you trust me with all this information instead of my dad or Aunt Alba, who is the eldest in the family. I'm sure she would know how to act or what to say."

"Perla, the day you asked me if you could stay with me while the pandemic passed, you told me you wanted to take the opportunity to learn more about the family. You mentioned that you felt distant, especially in recent years, because your busy daily life in Colorado didn't give you much time. You told me you were convinced that things happen at the exact moment and time they need to happen. That happened, dear; you came here with a purpose you yourself didn't know. Although you didn't know it, that purpose was to free me from this burden I've carried in my heart for more than thirty years, a feeling that hasn't let me rest, especially now, as I feel my life fading, and I don't want it to fade having that debt with my family, especially with Gabo."

"Oh, Bella, Bella Martini, all this time talking about the family, anecdotes, beautiful moments we all shared; we have talked so much... I even told you that I was writing a journal myself, including your stories. Now I'm surprised to think that you, years ago, had done the same, writing a journal, even in crucial moments that coincided with important dates in my journal, with the difference of several years apart. Everything I want to tell you crosses my mind at this moment, and I don't know where to start. I'm astonished at how much you and I resemble each other by the details I can read in your journal. There's something I want to mention before it slips my mind: it's incredible how you describe Rafael in your journal. When you talk about his details, it seems like I'm seeing Dad in them, with his slow way of speaking, his education and elegance in behavior, even his way of dressing, and his scent is exactly the same as I have described Dad countless times. That was something that caught my attention from the beginning of the journal; I never would have thought the story would end this way."

"It's true, Perla. Rafael and your dad are very similar in many things. It's as if, no matter how much I wanted to forget everything that happened when I came to this country, life reminded me of it with Gabo in every gesture, his gaze, his smile... The more the years passed and Gabo grew older, the more the similarities between them became evident."

"Now, what should I do with all this information, Bella? Where should I start? From what we are talking about, I understand that you want the family to know the truth and for me to be the one to start telling the story. Tell me, how do you think I should begin?"

November 25, 2020

If you've never embraced someone, begging life not to take them away, then you still don't know what it truly means to love.

We are celebrating Thanksgiving Day, a very important holiday in the United States, celebrated every year on the fourth Thursday of November. It is very common for people to travel around the country during this time to return to their hometowns or where they have more family, as it is customary during these dates to gather in homes for dinner together.

Given the current circumstances with the coronavirus, things are happening differently since the alert for infections is still in place here and around the world.

The Martini family will have dinner at the rented house with my aunts and my cousin. Naturally, Mr. Marlei won't be missing, and they've prepared a special chicken soup for him so he can celebrate with us tonight. The day has been beautiful, so my aunts have decided we will have dinner in the garden of the house. They have put a lot of effort into the decoration. They sent me a picture a few minutes ago, and everything is perfect. This time, they even told us not to bring any food, not even dessert, because they have been cooking for this date for a few days now.

On the other hand, Bella woke up a bit tired today as she had a rough night. I was worried, thinking I might have something to do with that tiredness since I haven't stopped gathering information to help me understand everything read in my grandmother's journal for the past two days. For this reason, I asked her to rest. She went to lie down after chatting a bit at breakfast, and I haven't felt her wake up yet.

After a while, I called Aunt Alba since we'd been trying to find time to talk for several days now. We have an important matter pending, and we can't delay it any longer.

"Good morning, Perla, dear. I'm glad we can finally match our time to chat; we've been postponing this important conversation for days."

"Yes, Aunt, it's true, but now that the moment has arrived, I don't want to beat around the bush. I want to talk about the text I sent you in an image to your cell phone two days ago. I suppose you could tell it was from Bella's journal. I think I've mentioned that I've been reading it, right?"

"Yes, of course, Perla. How could I not realize that those writings were my mother's handwriting? I was able to connect the dots with the names and descriptions that appeared on the page you sent me in the photo. I understood that it was the moment when Bella went to the doctor for a check-up because she suspected she was pregnant. From the date, I knew it would be your father. But tell me: What worries you so much about that, Perla?"

"Aunt, up until that moment, everything regarding the story of her pregnancy was normal. What I read days later is what prompted this call."

"And what did you read, Perla?"

"I don't know where to start telling you this. It's hard for me, but I'll try to be direct. Aunt, Dad is not the son of who we think he is; his real father is Rafael."

"Rafael? Rafael, Paloma's father? Where did you get that from, dear?"

"Aunt, I read it in her journal, but I also confirmed it with Bella. We've talked these days about what I've read in that journal, and indeed all that is true. Rafael is Dad's real father. I have a lot to tell you, but basically, Bella has lied about this all this time, and now she's asked me to be the one to talk to Dad about this truth. Bella doesn't believe she has the strength to do it, much less explain everything in detail, but she's willing to resolve any doubts the family might have about this topic once they know."

"Mmm…"

"Aunt? Are you there? Hello…?"

"Perla, I'm here; just give me a minute. Let me process all this."

"I'm sorry, Aunt, I don't want to spoil your Thanksgiving dinner; in fact, I never wanted to be the bearer of such news, but circumstances have led to this, and I've promised Bella that I will help her with this situation. She trusts me, and I won't let her down."

"That's true, dear. Bella has trusted you, and she was right to do so; I'm also convinced that you won't let her down. But, Perla, I ask that you give me a day and let me process everything you've told me today. Give me until tomorrow to understand everything. Don't worry, I trust you too, and I won't let you down, much less Bella. Just one thing before hanging up."

"Of course, Aunt, tell me."

"I must confess, Perla, that although this news is new to me, I always suspected something since the story of my mom being pregnant with Eduardo never quite added up for me. If, during those last months of pregnancy, he barely appeared at home, I also didn't entirely believe the story that we left Peru as a happy family because of a job offered to Eduardo, and upon arriving in New York, the job suddenly disappeared. Moreover, a few months after arriving, Bella decided we would move to New Jersey, but alone, without Eduardo. After that, I began to suspect that Eduardo had a different relationship with José, with whom he lived many years after our departure. Later, I learned that José died in New York from a rare disease that I didn't know or understand back then, but over time, I realized it was AIDS.

This news confirmed that my suspicions about the whole story of Mom, Eduardo, and José were correct, but I never dared to investigate or even ask. You know that I was always the one by Bella's side in her most difficult moments; I was her engine, so how could I stop to connect any dots if doing so would endanger my mother's machine? Later, little by little, when I began to take the course of my own life, the suspicions were left behind, buried as I got caught up in my own problems, which, as you know, haven't been few. Now, all those memories of my doubts flood my mind, and I need time to sort this out. Let tonight pass, please. I'll call you tomorrow at this time to talk better. Does that sound good?"

"Of course, Aunt, no problem. I'll wait for your call then."

"Perla, thank you for being who you are and for loving us so much! From the day I met you, I knew you would be the light of this family. I suffered with you through the loss of your mother. I would have given anything to avoid that moment for you, dear, but I couldn't do more; what I could do was take care of you, be by your side, and love you. You are, for all of us, the noble, brave, and loving woman we are proud of; don't forget that for a second."

* * *

May 21, 1967

My first son has been born. From the moment they told me it would be a boy, I decided to name him Gabriel. We waited for him so long, and he is finally with us. His sisters are excited about his arrival. This afternoon, when they came to meet him, they were jumping and shouting with joy. He is so beautiful, and when hungry, he desperately cries as if he hasn't eaten in a long time. His small face, slanted eyes, cherry-red lips, long fingers—everything about him reminds me of his father; he looks so much like him that there would be no way to deny it. However, for now, only Eduardo and I know the truth. I don't know how I'm going to bring up this topic yet; I need to think carefully about how I will tell the story to my daughters, to Rafael, and to Gabriel himself. I believe I won't confess the truth for some time. I know it's not the right thing to do, but for now, I'll leave it like this, waiting for the right moment, which I am sure will come soon.

* * *

December 11, 2020

Today, the United States Food and Drug Administration (FDA) approved the first COVID-19 vaccine. The vaccine is known as the "Pfizer BioNTech COVID-19 Vaccine" and will now be marketed under the name "Comirnaty" for the prevention of the disease in people aged sixteen and older.

We started the day with this news. We received a call from the hospital where Bella's primary care doctor works, informing us that they are awaiting the shipment of the Pfizer vaccines mentioned in the media. They trust that these will arrive at the hospital in the coming days, so they invited my grandmother to register on the list of the most vulnerable people so that as soon as they arrive, they will call her. This news has left us quite hopeful at home, as it means that somehow and little by little, the pandemic situation, which has been exhausting for everyone, is being controlled.

I spoke to Dad early in the day with the idea of telling him something, at least giving him a hint of what I've been thinking about these days, but I couldn't. He surprised me with the news that he would come to spend the Christmas holidays at the rented house with my aunts and, of course, with us. So, I decided that telling him over the phone about such a delicate topic was not the right way. I preferred to wait until he was here and could tell him everything calmly in a more personal conversation.

The good news about the vaccine and Gabo's return was overshadowed a bit in the afternoon when I talked to Solomon. Days ago, I had decided to be honest with him and open my heart. Did I really want to start something with him? Or, in general, could I start something with anyone at this moment? I took a few days to answer this question, and now that I had it clear, I felt it was my duty to talk to Solomon, as I saw him becoming more interested in what we were starting together. I decided to send him a text message to check if he was free for coffee and chat. I received his response, giving me a time and an address to meet at a café with a beautiful terrace near the hospital, where we could have more than just coffee.

"Hello, Perla. How are you? Please sit down. I've ordered something to eat; I'm very hungry today. I haven't eaten anything since yesterday afternoon; work at the hospital is killing me. I hope you like what I've ordered because it's quite a lot, and I need your help to eat it."

"Thank you, Solomon. You shouldn't have. I'm not very hungry, but I'll join you with something to drink. Let me see the menu."

"Of course, Perla, as you wish, don't worry. But tell me, how have you been?

"Everything is fine at home; thanks for asking, Solomon, but actually, I wanted to talk to you about another topic."

"What happened, Perla? You're scaring me. Is everything okay?

"Well, I'd like to start by thanking you for everything we've shared so far. It's been a privilege to know you."

"Perla, it sounds like you're saying goodbye."

"Please, let me finish, Solomon. What I have to tell you isn't easy. I've thought about it a lot, but everything I've learned in these months here with Bella, with you, and with everything, in general, has shown me that things happen at the exact moment they are meant to happen. Knowing you helped me understand that what I had with Javier wasn't what I really thought; even though it sounds strange, you showed me what I want in life for myself as a partner. It's hard to say all this, but it's true: you are a gentleman, a noble, loving man with values similar to mine who loves and respects his family, is altruistic, and is eager to make a mark in this world. That's what I understood since I was a child that I wanted for myself, but along the way, I lost my direction.

Today, Solomon, I have decided to find myself again, to take the time to heal, to heal my wounds, to gather my strength, and to rise dressed in self-love to shine again. Only then I will be ready to start something with someone. I don't know how long this will take. I also don't know if by then you will still be free or interested in me. The only thing I know for sure is that I need this; I owe it to myself, and I'm going to do it. I'm sure I will find myself in a different stage, grown and mature. Only then will I seek love in another person when what I have to give is peace, and I exactly know what I want for myself."

"Perla, what you're telling me catches me by surprise. I didn't expect it but don't worry, I understand what you're saying. It seems very valid. You indeed need that time. You are a wonderful woman, and you deserve a man like the one you hope for, like the one you've always dreamed of. Take the time you need to achieve your goal, and don't worry about me. I just hope with all my heart that when you are ready, our paths will cross again, and we will both be available for things to happen. This is not a goodbye; I trust in that."

December 17, 2020

The moment I had been dreading these past few weeks has arrived: Gabo landed yesterday at Fort Lauderdale Airport in Florida but went straight to a hotel until today when he was able to take a COVID-19 test to ensure he arrived from Colombia without the virus.

When he arrived home, the first thing he did was call me to meet up; I told him to wait for me at the rented house and that I would stop by. So, I did. I went alone with Mr. Marlei under the pretense of taking him for a walk to be able to talk along the way.

After greeting each other with a long hug and asking about Marta, who I knew had arrived exhausted from the trip, we went out to walk Mr. Marlei.

"How long will you be staying, Dad?"

"We'll be here all of December and January. We plan to return in early February, but we don't have confirmed tickets yet, so don't worry, dear; you'll have your dad around for a good while."

"That's great, Gabo. You'll cheer us up these days, as always. But tell me, how is everything in Cartagena?"

"Everything is fine, Perla, my love, but forgive me for changing the subject so abruptly. You know I'm your dad, and I know you. I can tell something has been bothering you for some days now. I've noticed it during our phone conversations. Tell me, daughter, is there something you want to share?"

"Dad, you're right. I'm sorry I haven't been able to tell you this before, but I preferred to wait and do it in person."

"Perla, you're worrying me."

"Let's sit here, Dad, come. Don't worry, I'm going to tell you everything, but sit down because it's quite a story. Do you remember Bella's diary, Dad, the one she gave me for my birthday and that I've been reading all these months, which we've often discussed?"

"Yes, of course, Perla. How could I forget? That diary has brought back many memories of my mother's life, some happy and others not so much. We've even gotten melancholic thinking about everything Bella went through back then."

"Well, Gabo, it turns out I haven't managed to discuss the end of the diary with you."

"Perla, dear, you scared me. I thought it was something terrible happening to you or Bella."

"Dad, wait, please let me talk. There's a lot I need to tell you still. I finished my grandmother's diary, and, almost at the end, I found something our family wasn't aware of—news that affects all of us, but especially you. I have the diary with me, and I'd like to read something to you because I think it will help me tell you everything since talking about it is proving difficult for me.

I can't believe what you're telling me now. What great news! You know I'd love for you and the girls to join us. We can start a whole new life far from here. I have very advanced plans; let me give you the details so you can see the plan is foolproof.

Before you give me more information, I want to tell you something, Eduardo. I'm pregnant; I realized a few days ago that I hadn't had my period for over two months. With all the craziness happening these days, that detail slipped my mind. As soon as I realized it, I rushed to the doctor, who confirmed I was expecting a baby. I'm pregnant, and the baby is Rafael's. Neither he nor anyone else can know. We'll say the baby is yours and that we're moving to America because you have a job offer you can't refuse, so we'll plan our departure as soon as possible.

We'll also say José is coming with us since he, too, has been hired by the same company that gave you the job. Once we arrive in the United States, we'll see how things develop and the direction each of us must take. Eduardo, I want to make it clear that saying we're going together is just to avoid raising suspicions about my pregnancy, nothing more. You know you owe me this. You'll do it, right?"

When I finished reading the diary and closed it, I noticed my father's face was drenched in tears. I remember, as a child, seeing my father cry desperately through the crack in the door without being able to console him, and a cold sensation ran through my body.

"I'm so sorry, Gabo. I never wanted something like this to happen, much less to be the one to tell you this story. Forgive me, Dad."

"How long have you known this, Perla?"

"As I told you, I reached the end of the diary a few days ago, and this came up in those last pages. As soon as I read the end, I asked Bella to talk about it. She pleaded for me to be the one to speak with you. As we all know, Bella, at ninety years old, doesn't have the same strength she once did, and dealing with this truth is difficult for her, Gabo. But it was clear she couldn't leave without telling you what she had hidden for so long. I know I can't fully understand what you're feeling because I'm not the one going through this, but I've tried to put myself in your shoes before talking to you. It hurts to see you go through such pain, but this isn't the first pain we've faced together, and it might not be the last. I'm here with you, Dad. I don't have more words to say, but I want you to know I'm here, and I'll stay here for you."

We sat on that bench for the next thirty minutes without speaking. I just watched Gabo cry like a child, hugging my lap. I couldn't talk, only console him by stroking his head and wiping his tears with whatever I could until it started to rain, and Mr. Marlei cried, scared of the downpour. At that moment, we headed back to the rented house.

When we arrived home, no one asked what was wrong, as they suspected something. Aunt Alondra simply received him with a hug, which collapsed Dad; she just held him, letting him cry deeply.

I returned home with a profound sadness as images of my father came to mind when I was a child, hearing him question why life had taken his family away. Although this time I had the strength to hug him and tell him I was there for him, still, my heart felt it, and I wished none of this had happened to him again.

December 24, 2020

Everything that has happened these past few days has been like an emotional rollercoaster. In general, I think since the pandemic began or since the moment I boarded the plane in Colorado and landed in Florida, my life has taken a 360-degree turn.

We are about to close a new year, a year I started without having any idea of everything that would happen in my life and in the lives of everyone around me. I thought that by staying to live with Bella, I would be helping her cope with the pandemic and her illness, but it ended up being her and everyone around her who showed me the vastly different direction my life would take from the first day I arrived at her house. I don't complain; on the contrary, it has been much better than I ever thought it would be, including the uncertain moments we all went through, as they made me value today as the most precious gift life has given me.

I can't help but quickly summarize what has happened in the Martini family in these last few days.

Dad, after a few days of meditation on what he had just discovered, finally decided to talk to Bella. She was able to answer all his questions. At the end of their conversation, not without having cried until they were dry, they embraced in a healing hug that let go of all the fears and doubts that had haunted them. Dad forgave my grandmother's silence and lie, though it didn't stop hurting him. I feel he's still in that process. Afterward, Dad set out to find Eduardo, whom we had lost track of years ago for a thousand reasons that I won't recount now and that may be the subject of another diary. Finally, we found out yesterday that Dad managed to locate Eduardo; they talked a lot, and Dad confessed that he now knew the truth.

Eduardo, for his part, currently lives alone in Manhattan, New York, in a small apartment he bought from his work as a chef in several of the city's most famous restaurants. He always liked cooking and had the talent to make each dish a work of art.

Solomon sent a bouquet home accompanied by a beautiful card for the holidays, in which he wrote a message wishing us happy holidays in his own handwriting. I haven't stopped being in touch with him via text messages. While it's true that our communication isn't very continuous, we write to each other every two or three days to remind each other that we are there if we need each other.

Aunt Paloma, Uncle Vicente, and Vicente Jr. are happy because a few days ago, Antonio arrived to spend Christmas and New Year's Eve with us. The whole family together is a luxury; everyone talks and laughs at the same time. It was a wonderful concert that I enjoyed a lot. Antonio's birthday is coming up in the next few days, so we're also organizing a nice family gathering after Christmas to celebrate his birthday. I'm sure Antonio will surprise us that night, as he always does, with his wonderful singing and guitar playing.

Aunt Alondra, along with her husband, Stefano, and my cousin Mathías, have spent beautiful days enjoying the family at the rented house, where they have gifted us with nights of conversation and delicious meals, but most of all, they have left us filled with love, the love they always reflect and that we appreciate so much. Today, they are in charge of preparing Christmas Eve dinner.

Dad, Marta, and I are in charge of the desserts for dinner. Everything is turning out perfect because today we are going to celebrate not only Christmas Eve but also the Martini family and its value as a family. We also celebrate Bella, who, with her inexhaustible love, has managed to overcome all the trials life has thrown at her, making it possible for her to enjoy today what she has built with so much effort, courage, and dedication.

And me? I've decided to return to Colorado. Flights have resumed almost regularly across the country, and I've started looking for an apartment. I have several appointments to view them in the first days of January. I'm going to take charge of the clinic again and start attending more regularly in person. I also have some conversations with colleagues about bringing our clinics to virtual platforms to reach many more people across the country, taking advantage of our positive experience with virtual appointments during the pandemic and the excellent results we achieved in those months.

Regarding love, as I told Solomon, I'm processing everything that happened with Javier, with whom I reconnected to close our pending relationship issues. I found him quite calm, which I liked a lot. I sincerely wish Javier finds love with the girl he's now seeing. I know he wants to start a family soon, and I hope he succeeds. He deserves to be happy.

As for Solomon, for now, I'm going to be alone. I'm not closing myself off to anything in the future, but I need to sort out my life, resume my professional career in Colorado, and organize my short-term plans.

So, I think this diary has reached its end on this page. When I started writing it, I never imagined everything that would happen here. How crazy! I'm sure if someone had told me, I would have laughed, saying those wild and crazy things don't happen to me, that my life is very predictable, and everything is organized in the best way. Now I understand that nothing is like that.

"Perla, come! It's time to open the presents. We want to do it before dinner," my cousin Mathías shouted.

Alondra grabbed an envelope without knowing who it was from or for and read aloud:

From Bella to Perla, with all my heart.

"Open it! Open it!" everyone shouted in chorus.

Perla, this gift is incredibly special because I know it's something you were thinking of doing but were waiting for the right moment. I think it can help you understand that the moment has arrived.

Said the card accompanying the envelope.

It was a certificate with round-trip tickets for two people for fifteen days, with paid accommodation to Lima, Peru, as well as several tours included to get to know the city, a place I had never visited, though I always had the idea in mind.

"Dad, this gift is ours; we owe it to ourselves. We will go next year; we will both see the country where Bella was so happy, and we will look for your family together."

THE END